Mayan Mythology for Teens

Enthralling Tales and Cosmic Myths from Ancient Mesoamerica

© Copyright 2025 - All rights reserved.

The content contained within this book may not be reproduced, duplicated, or transmitted without direct written permission from the author or the publisher.

Under no circumstances will any blame or legal responsibility be held against the publisher, or author, for any damages, reparation, or monetary loss due to the information contained within this book, either directly or indirectly.

Legal Notice:

This book is copyright protected. It is only for personal use. You cannot amend, distribute, sell, use, quote, or paraphrase any part, or the content within this book, without the consent of the author or publisher.

Disclaimer Notice:

Please note the information contained within this document is for educational and entertainment purposes only. All effort has been executed to present accurate, up-to-date, reliable, and complete information. No warranties of any kind are declared or implied. Readers acknowledge that the author is not engaging in the rendering of legal, financial, medical, or professional advice. The content within this book has been derived from various sources. Please consult a licensed professional before attempting any techniques outlined in this book.

By reading this document, the reader agrees that under no circumstances is the author responsible for any losses, direct or indirect, that are incurred as a result of the use of the information contained within this document, including, but not limited to, errors, omissions, or inaccuracies.

Free limited time bonus

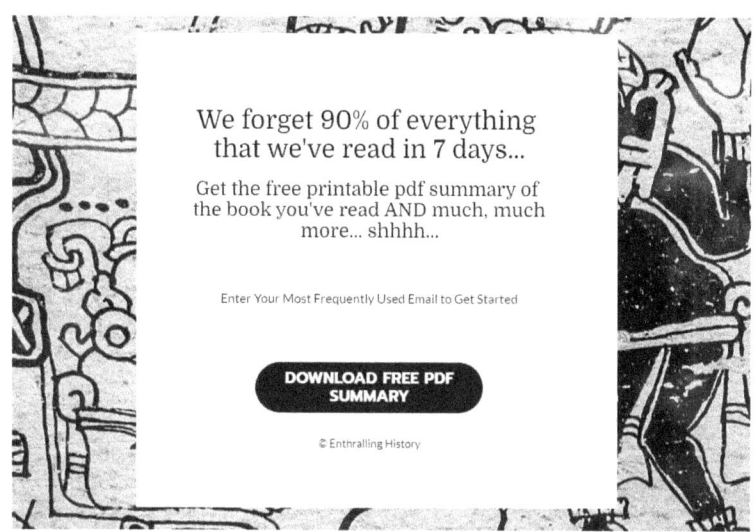

Stop for a moment. We have a free bonus set up for you. The problem is this: we forget 90% of everything that we read after 7 days. Crazy fact, right? Here's the solution: we've created a printable, 1-page pdf summary for this book that you're reading now. All you have to do to get your free pdf summary is to go to the following website: https://livetolearn.lpages.co/enthrallinghistory/

Or, Scan the QR code!

Once you do, it will be intuitive. Enjoy, and thank you!

Table of Contents

INTRODUCTION 1
PRONUNCIATION GUIDE 3
CHAPTER 1: THE MAYA CREATION STORY 5
CHAPTER 2: THE MAYA PANTHEON 16
CHAPTER 3: THE HERO TWINS AND THE UNDERWORLD 27
CHAPTER 4: UNLOCKING THE MAYA CALENDAR 43
CHAPTER 5: GLYPHS OF POWER: READING THE ANCIENT SCRIPTS 53
CHAPTER 6: TIKAL, THE CITY OF GODS 63
CHAPTER 7: BELIEFS, RITUALS, AND THE CYCLE OF LIFE AND DEATH 74
CHAPTER 8: SHAMANS AND THEIR MAGIC 84
CHAPTER 9: MAYA MYSTERIES AND MAGICAL FOLKTALES 91
CHAPTER 10: MORE EXCITING EXPLOITS OF THE HERO TWINS 104
ANSWERS TO ROUNDUP QUESTIONS 115
HERE'S ANOTHER BOOK BY ENTHRALLING HISTORY THAT YOU MIGHT LIKE 124
FREE LIMITED TIME BONUS 125
BIBLIOGRAPHY 126
IMAGE SOURCES 128

Introduction

Do you love tortillas? You can thank the early Maya of Guatemala, who invented them around 3,500 years ago. They covered maize (corn) with water and threw in a chunk of hot limestone. When the Maya soaked the corn like this, they could grind it, form a dough, and make tortillas. This *nixtamalization* process spread throughout *Mesoamerica* (the region from central Mexico to Costa Rica).

What do tortillas have to do with mythology? Tales of corn (or maize) weave throughout Maya mythology. It symbolized life and abundance, and the maize god represented resurrection. The Maya gods created humans from tortilla dough. The Maya believed their ancestors were gods who taught them how to grow corn and make tortillas, their primary food.

The Maya adopted simple writing, bouncy rubber balls, and chocolate from the Olmec culture. Yet, they took it all to the next level. It wasn't long before spectacular Maya cities sprang up in southern Mexico, the Yucatán Peninsula, Belize, Guatemala, Honduras, and El Salvador. The Maya never formed a united empire, but they shared a similar culture and the Mayan language family.

Speaking of language, is it "Maya" or "Mayan?" We use *"Mayan"* for the language and *"Maya"* for the people and culture.

Instead of an empire, the Maya had independent *city-states*. These large, major cities ruled over the small towns and farm villages surrounding them. Each city-state had its own king, who the Maya thought was part human and part god. The Maya rulers constantly fought other cities for things like chocolate, quetzal bird feathers, and trade routes. They also needed victims for human sacrifice, which their gods required. The first Maya city-state was Kaminaljuyú, which had ceramic factories by 800 BCE. Its ruins are under Guatemala City's western suburbs.

Sometimes, a city-state formed a mini-empire by conquering nearby cities. The losers had to pay tribute and provide men for its army. *Tribute* is something like a tax on conquered people. Sometimes, they paid with cacao (chocolate beans), which was "money" for the Maya. They also paid with currency like bird feathers, cotton, rubber balls, and seashells.

How do we know what we know about ancient Maya mythology? Fortunately, two important books survived the Spaniards' book burning. The *Popol Vuh* has stories of creation and how the Maya began. It tells how the "Hero Twins" battled monsters and competed in a sacred ball game in the underworld. *Chilam Balam* (*The Book of the Jaguar Priest*) has ancient Maya myths, religious rituals, and history. The Maya believed some of their priests could see into the future. Some foretold the Spanish invasion in the *Chilam Balam*.

What's the point of learning mythology? It helps us understand a people's identity. For example, what was most important to the Maya? How did they perceive the universe and the passing of time? Who were their most important gods, and how did the Maya worship them? What stories did they have about their gods and supernatural events? Let's explore the frequently freakish yet mesmerizing Maya mythology.

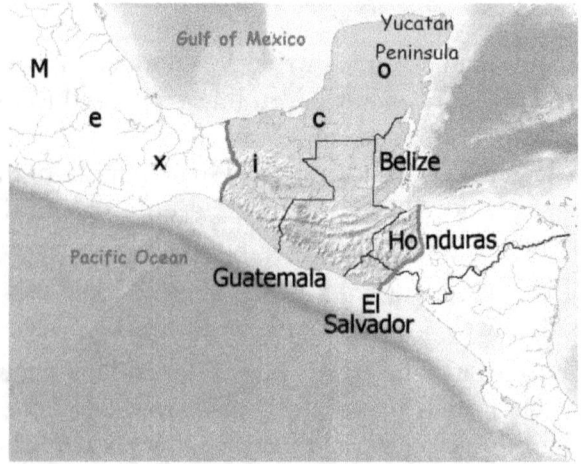

Map of Maya Territory[1]

Pronunciation Guide

The Mayan language family has over twenty-eight languages spoken by six million Maya today, around the same number as before the Spanish takeover. Here is an essential guide for pronouncing K'iche' (Quiché), the largest Mayan language sub-group. About one million Maya speak K'iche' in Guatemala today.

Remember these guidelines for consonants and vowels that are different from English:

1. Pronounce "b'" like you're swallowing the sound.
2. Pronounce "ch'" like in "chair" but with a pop of air.
3. Pronounce "j" with a raspy "h" sound, as in "jalapeño."
4. Pronounce "k'" like "k" but with a pop of air.
5. Pronounce "q" like "k" but in the back of your throat.
6. Pronounce "r" like a Spanish single "r" (no roll) with the tip of your tongue on the roof of your mouth.
7. Pronounce "tz" like the sound at the end of "cats."
8. Pronounce "x" with a "sh" sound, as in "shell."
9. Pronounce "a" with an "ah" sound, as in "father."
10. Pronounce "aa" with a prolonged "ahhhh" sound.
11. Pronounce "ä" like "uh," as in "about."
12. Pronounce "ay" like "eye."
13. Pronounce "e" with a short "ay" sound, as in "gate."

14. Pronounce "ee" with a prolonged "aaay" sound.
15. Pronounce "ey" like you would in "they."
16. Pronounce "i" with an "ee" sound, as in "police."
17. Pronounce "ii" with a prolonged "eeee" sound.
18. Pronounce "o" with a long "oh" sound, as in "show."
19. Pronounce "oo" with a prolonged "oh" sound.
20. Pronounce "oy" like you would in "boy."
21. Pronounce "u" with a long "u" sound, as in "flute."
22. Pronounce "uu" with a prolonged "u" sound.
23. Pronounce "uy" like the "uoy" in "buoy."

Chapter 1: The Maya Creation Story

How did the world, people, and sun come to be, according to ancient Maya mythology? The Maya creation myth is in the *Popol Vuh*, a book that contains stories of the K'iche' Maya history and mythology. It explains how the gods tried several times to create people and failed. Finally, they got it right. It also tells how human sacrifice began and how languages divided.

Who Wrote the *Popol Vol*?

The Spaniards first arrived in Guatemala in 1524 CE. Their brutal conquest of the Maya stretched until 1697. In this period, 85 percent of the Maya died from war, harsh slavery, and diseases against which they had no immunity. Guatemala's highland Maya were among the first to fall to Spanish rule. Shortly after, Dominican and Franciscan friars arrived to convert them to Catholicism. They set up schools to teach the boys and young men of elite families how to read and write in the alphabet that we use now.

Some young Maya noblemen from the town of Chichicastenango in Guatemala's highlands began transcribing their ancient books into the modern alphabet. They aimed to preserve their ancient history and legends, as the Spaniards discouraged the Maya hieroglyphics and burned their ancient books. These K'iche' writers said the *Popol Vuh* was an "instrument of sight," enabling the readers to see their ancestors' and gods' actions and thoughts. This "sight" stretched back to the beginning of time and forward into the future.

The Maya elders kept the *Popol Vuh* hidden from the Spaniards for two centuries. Finally, a Dominican priest in Chichicastenango, Guatemala, named Francisco Ximénez, won the Maya's trust. The K'iche' told him about the ancient book they had hidden away. Ximénez translated the *Popol Vuh* into Spanish. He wrote that K'iche' parents taught their children the stories while they were still breastfeeding. Most of the K'iche' in his region knew the *Popol Vuh* by heart.

Pyramid at Chichén Itzá'

The Maya had lived in Guatemala's mountains for thousands of years. Several centuries before the Spaniards arrived, the Nahuatl-speaking Toltecs of central Mexico had fled to Chichén Itzá in the Yucatán Peninsula when their kingdom crumbled in the twelfth century. Other Toltecs had already settled there by 1000 CE. Before the Toltecs, Maya records say the Teotihuacanos of central Mexico invaded in 378 CE. As a result of these influences, the Maya retained the essence of their culture but added in Teotihuacan, Toltec, and eventually Aztec characteristics. They all shared the feathered serpent god that the K'iche' called Tepeu Q'ukumatz (Kukulkan) and the Toltecs and Aztecs called Quetzalcoatl.

What Was the *Popol Vol* Creation Myth?

The *Popol Vuh* writers wrote the creation myth in the present tense as if the action were unfolding as the story progressed. Here it is:

This is the story of the dawn brought by the divine mother and father, Grandmother Xmucane (the Maker) and Grandfather Xpiyacoc (the

Builder). These two are the oldest gods. It is also the story of Tepew (the Sovereign), Q'ukumatz (the Feathered Serpent), and Huracán (the Hurricane).

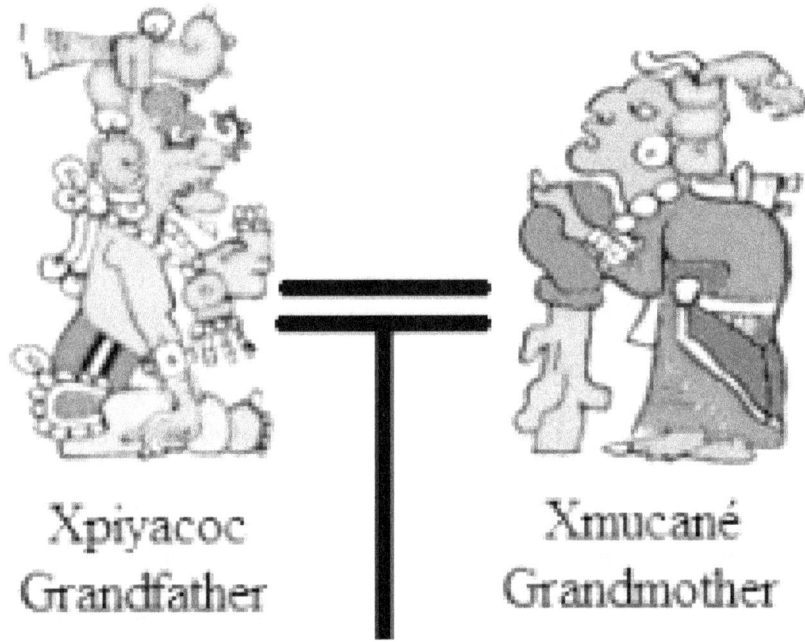

The oldest gods, Xpiyacoc and Xmucane'

In the beginning, everything is dark and silent. The empty sky hangs over the sea's expanse. The land has not yet appeared. Maker, Builder, Sovereign, Feathered Serpent, and Hurricane meet in the darkness. They talk, ponder, and agree.

Their word creates the Earth. They say, "Earth," and it appears. They call the mountains out of the water. They create cypress groves and pine forests to cover the mountains and valleys. They make rivers flow from the mountains.

"Everything we have made is good!" they all agree.

The First Animals

Maker and Builder frown. "Is everything going to be silent and lonely beneath the trees?"

So, they create animals as guardians of the mountains and forests. They make the birds, deer, jaguar, puma, and rattlesnake. They tell them to multiply.

Yet, Maker and Builder are dissatisfied with the animals. "Speak! Say our names! Worship us! We are your mother and father!"

Yet, the animals can only roar, squawk, growl, and chatter. They can't speak. They can't worship their creators.

The creators scold the animals, "You can't speak successfully. You can't say our names and worship us. Therefore, we will create someone else to honor and worship us. Your destiny is to be food. You will be killed and eaten. You will serve the one we shall create to worship us."

Maker and Builder look at each other. "Before the dawn approaches, let's try to make a worshiper who will honor, respect, and provide for us."

Two Bungled Attempts to Create People

They form a man from the mud, but the mud crumbles. It is too mushy. The mud man's face can't turn. He only looks in one direction. The mud man speaks, but he doesn't make sense. Then, his face dissolves, and the mud man falls apart.

Maker and Builder look at each other. "This mud man is a mistake! He can't walk. He can't reproduce. Let's move on and leave this useless thing behind."

After they knock the mud man over, they wonder, "How can we make someone who will worship us, say our names, and have children?"

As they ponder their problem, Hurricane, Feathered Serpent, and Sovereign join them. "Grandmother and Grandfather, we should chisel new people out of wood."

Q'ukumatz (Kukulkan), the Feathered Serpent*

The gods cut down a coral tree and carve its wood into the shape of a man. They take reeds and make a woman. The people speak! They give birth to sons and daughters. However, they still have a problem. They don't have hearts and minds. Without minds, they cannot remember

Grandmother Maker and Grandfather Builder. They forget Hurricane and the other gods. They are incapable of understanding. Their skin has no oil or sweat, so their faces dry up, and they stop speaking. No blood flows inside them, so their arms and legs are stiff and shriveled. They can't even walk. Instead, they crawl on their hands and knees.

The gods weigh the humans in the balance. "They are no good! They're just an experiment. This second attempt at making people has failed."

The gods decide to send *Butic*, the flood of judgment. Hurricane brings the flood down on the heads of the people. A black rain falls day and night, and the flood kills them. Death Knives cuts off their heads. Crouching Jaguar eats them. Striking Jaguar smashes their bones and tendons. They grind up their bones. The dogs and turkeys speak to the humans, "You caused us pain. You ate us! Now, we're eating you!"

Seven Macaw and the Twins

The wooden humans that survive the flood become the spider monkeys in the forest. After the flood, the world still has no sun or moon. Meanwhile, the bird god, Seven Macaw, proudly puffs himself up at his glorious appearance. "I am a bright sign for those who died in the flood. My essence is enchanted! I am the sun and the moon! I light the people's paths with my glittering gold and silver. My eyes are brilliant green jewels."

In reality, Seven Macaw isn't a powerful god. He can't actually shine like the sun. The twin gods, Hunahpu and Xbalanque, hear him. They disapprove of Seven Macaw's pride. Hunahpu is a great hunter and blowgun master. His brother Xbalanque is ferocious like the jaguar. They frown as they look at Seven Macaw.

"No good will come of this! People can't live here if he's trying to be the sun! Let's shoot Seven Macaw with our blowguns."

Each young god shoulders his blowgun. They learn that Seven Macaw has two sons by his wife, Chimalmat. His son Zipacna claims that he is the creator and guardian of the six volcanoes that exist at that time. The other son, Cabracan, is like an earthquake, shaking the mountains and making them spit lava.

"I'm the creator of the Earth!" Zipacna brags.

"Well, I'm the one who makes the sky fall! I shake the volcanoes and make them collapse," boasts Cabracan.

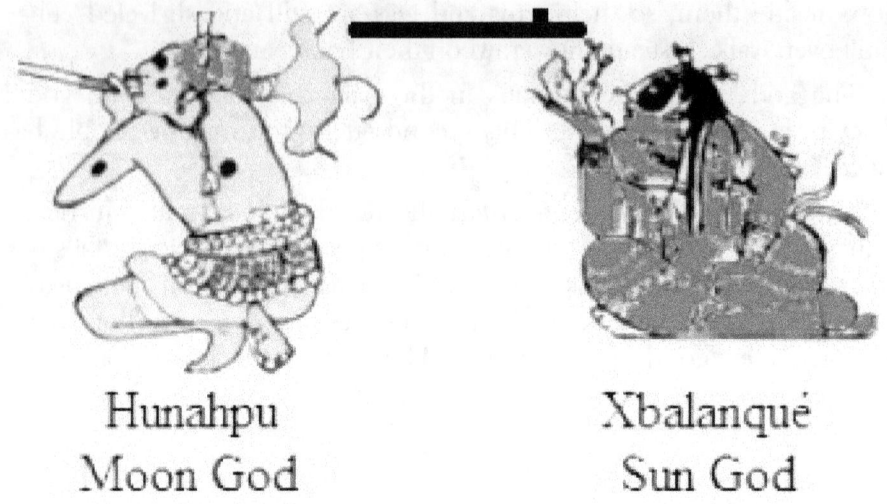

Hunahpu
Moon God

Xbalanqué
Sun God

The Twins'

When Hunahpu and Xbalanque hear this, they realize the boys have the same sin as their father, Seven Macaw. "Their evil pride will harm the world. We need to kill them, too!" the twins decide.

Seven Macaw loves the small golden fruit of the nance tree. Every morning, he flies up to the top of the tree and knocks down some fruit. The twins hide underneath the tree, and Seven Macaw can't see them through the leaves. When the bird god lands on a branch just over their head, Hunahpu shoots a pellet at him from his blowgun. It strikes Seven Macaw in the jaw, and he screams in pain, falling out of the tree and landing on the ground.

Hunahpu runs over to grab him, but Seven Macaw is feisty. He grabs Hunahpu's arm and rips it off, flying back to his wife with the arm in his claws.

"What's that you've got there?" Chimalmat asks.

"Two demons shot their blowguns at me! Now my jaw is dislocated! I will hang this arm over the fire to roast until those demons come looking for it."

Meanwhile, the twins visit their ancient grandparents, white-haired and bent over with age. Their grandfather is Great White Peccary, and their grandmother is Great White Coati.

"Can you help us?" the twins ask. "Come with us to visit Seven Macaw so we can get Hunahpu's arm back. We'll stay behind you, and you do all the talking. Tell him we're orphans."

"Okay, let's go," their grandparents say. They disguise themselves as folk healers.

They arrive at Seven Macaw's tree, where he is loudly screaming because his jaw hurts so badly. When he sees the elderly couple, he asks, "Where did you come from, grandfather and grandmother?"

"Our lord, we're just making a living," the grandparents humbly answer.

"What kind of living?" Seven Macaw asks. "Are these your children behind you?"

"No, lord, they're our grandchildren. We take pity on them and give them our food scraps to eat."

Seven Macaw is about to faint with pain. His injured jaw makes it difficult to speak. "I beg you, take pity on me! Do you have any medicine to stop this pain in my jaw?"

"Our job is to repair teeth, set broken bones, and heal eye inflammation," the grandparents answer.

"Please, then," Seven Macaw groans, "heal my painful jaw and my eyes! Two demons shot me with their blowguns! I'm in anguish!"

"Okay, it's probably your teeth that are hurting. We'll take them out," the grandparents say.

"But I don't want to lose my teeth!" the bird god complains. "They are part of what makes me such a resplendent god."

"No worries. We'll replace them with this bone," the grandparents cheerfully answer. "Look how bright and shiny it is!"

However, it isn't really bone. It's white corn kernels. They remove all of Seven Macaw's beautiful teeth and replace them with maize kernels. Then they take out his eyes. Seven Macaw has no more pain, but he can't see. And he's no longer glorious; he's just ordinary. Soon, Seven Macaw dies because he can't see to fly and can't eat without teeth. Hunahpu gets his arm back, and his grandparents place it back into his arm socket.

What about Seven Macaw's sons, Zipacna and Cabracan? We'll unwrap that story in chapter ten. Chapter three unwraps the twins' famous ball game in the underworld. For now, let's return to the creator gods, who are still trying to create people.

The Gods Finally Succeed in Creating People

Grandmother Maker and Grandfather Builder meet with Feathered Serpent, Sovereign, and Hurricane. "It's almost dawn, and we still haven't finished our task! No humans are on the face of the Earth."

The gods put their heads together and sift through their thoughts. Suddenly, the answer is crystal clear! Four animals—fox, coyote, parakeet, and raven—show them fields of yellow and white corn at Mount Paxil. The corn will become the flesh of the new humans. The mountain has other treasures, such as cacao beans for making chocolate, honey, and every kind of fruit tree.

Grandmother Maker grinds the corn nine times to make a fine dust. They mix the corn flour with water to form dough and shape the new humans. The first four men have yellow skin from the corn. Their names are Jaguar Forest, Jaguar Night, Traveler, and Black Jaguar. They are the ancestors of the human race that lives today. They breathe, and life comes to them. They hear, speak, and see. They can walk and hold things with their hands. They can understand everything under the sky. Their eyesight is so keen they can see distant things without walking there, even on the other end of the Earth. They are excellently made.

Jaguar Forest, Jaguar Night, Traveler, and Black Jaguar turn toward the creator gods. "We thank you! We thank you! We thank you! We praise you for blessing us with mouths and ears so we can speak and listen. We thank you that we can think and walk around. Thank you for creating us, Grandmother and Grandfather!"

The gods are happy to receive the worship and praise of their new humans. Yet, they worry. "Their eyesight is *too* perfect. They can see everything! They can see all four corners of the Earth at once. They can even see into heaven. What if they grow proud? They'll think they're gods and won't reproduce and have children. They won't plant corn and grow crops. We had better undo things a little so our new humans won't get too proud."

Hurricane dims the new humans' eyesight so they can only see things nearby. They lose the great wisdom they had when they could see everything on Earth and in heaven. The first four men need wives, so the gods put them to sleep. When they wake up, each man has a beautiful wife. The men are overjoyed! Jaguar Forest's wife is Sea Turtle. Jaguar Night's wife is Shrimp. Traveler's wife is Hummingbird. Black Jaguar's wife is Macaw.

The People Desperately Search for the Sun

The gods have now satisfactorily created people who begin having children. Yet, they still have a problem. There is no sun! The people are walking around in the dark, bumping into each other. They begin walking east, instinctively feeling light might be in that direction. They search for the sun. They plead to their creator gods, yet they do not pray to idols of stone or wood. They only lift their faces to the sky. "Do not abandon us! Give us light!"

They fast and pray as they await the dawn. When no sun comes, they travel east to Tulan Zuyva, the land of the seven caves. By now, there are many K'iche' people, and they have formed three groups. At Tulan, each of the three groups receives a different god, an idol to carry with them. The three groups of the K'iche' people go their separate ways as they leave Tulan. Now, they speak different languages. They wear animal hides for clothing, but they do not yet have fire. Everything is still dark and cold.

A ceramic vessel, probably Tohil'

One of the three groups has the idol of the fire god Tohil. He speaks to them and gives them fire. They are grateful for its light and warmth, but it begins to rain down hail, and the fire goes out.

"Oh, Tohil! Give us fire, or we'll die of cold!" the K'iche' pray.

And he gives them fire again. But the other two tribes also want fire. They ask Tohil's group to share their fire, but they say no. The other people are shivering and crawl to Tohil's people on their hands and knees.

"Take pity on us! Give us just a little bit of your fire."

"What will you give us in return?" Tohil's group asks.

"We'll give you gold and silver!"

"We don't want precious metals. What else do you have?"

"Well, what do you want?" the desperate people ask.

"We're not sure. We need to ask our god Tohil."

When they ask Tohil, he says, "Tell them to give their hearts."

His followers pass on his demand to the tribes who want fire. They all submit, giving their hearts, and their blood flows from their chests. Now, they have fire, but they're dead. They have no hearts. Only Tohil's people can live and reproduce. The god tells his people to pierce their ears and let the blood drip to give thanks. The people obey him. One of them carries the idol of Tohil on his back as Tohil leads them to Mount Chi Pixab to await the dawn.

Food cannot grow without the sun, so the people are starving. They all wait on top of the mountain for the dawn. "First, you'll see the morning star. Then, the sun will arise!" Tohil promises them.

When they finally see the glittering morning star, they all rejoice. They unwrap their incense and burn it as tears stream down their faces. And then, the first ray pierces the sky as the sun is born. The people weep and hug each other as they watch the brilliant sun appear, giving light and warmth. The birds sing and fly around as the pumas and jaguars roar. The people kneel in thanksgiving. Yet, as the sun reaches the top of the sky, its heat is unbearable, and everyone looks for shade.

Roundup Activity: Comprehension Questions

Check your answers in the back of the book.

1. Why did the K'iche' Maya hide the *Popol Vuh* from the Spaniards for two centuries? Who translated it into Spanish?

2. Who were the two oldest gods in Maya mythology? What other three gods worked with them to create the world and people?

3. Why did the gods punish the animals?

4. What did the gods use to make humans in their first two unsuccessful tries?

5. What was the sin of Seven Macaw and his sons?

6. What did the gods finally use to create humans successfully?

7. What problem did the people have after they were created?

8. What god told the K'iche' people to sacrifice human hearts?

Chapter 2: The Maya Pantheon

The Maya had around 250 deities. All the Maya (and much of the rest of Mesoamerica) worshiped certain gods, like the rain god Chaac. Other gods were regional. As we saw in the last chapter, the Maya did not believe their gods were infallible or incapable of making mistakes. Nor did they think they were all-powerful. The gods only had superpowers in specific areas. Often, a god would ask another god for help. Maya gods were not infinite. Most of them were born at some point, like the Hero Twins. Many of them died, like Seven Macaw and the Hero Twins' father. Furthermore, the Maya called their kings "ajaw," or "divine lord," believing they were part human and part god.

This chapter provides an in-depth exploration of the rich and diverse pantheon of Maya gods. Each had a unique area over which he or she had control, such as agriculture, war, or weather. The Maya gods had essential roles in the cosmos but also interacted personally in people's lives. Let's check out the more well-known gods of the Maya and their roles. Many gods had several regional names because of the many languages in the Mayan language family. They also often had different names in Nahuatl (Aztec, Toltec) and other Mesoamerican languages.

Kukulkan, the Feathered Serpent (Tepeu Q'ukumatz, Gucumatz)

Most creator gods faded into the background once they finally created functional humans and a sun. However, the Feathered Serpent stayed active as a leading Maya god. He instructed the humans he helped create, teaching them how to grow crops, build things, hunt, and fish. He also taught them law, writing, medicine, and other knowledge needed for civilization. Other Mesoamerican cultures worshiped him, beginning in at least 100 CE in Teotihuacan.

Kukulkan was the god of wind and assisted his friend, Chaac, with providing rain. He was the fusion of Earth (serpent) and sky (feathers), representing fertility and regeneration.

Image of Kukulkan, the Feathered Serpent, at Chichén Itzá[7]

The El Castillo pyramid at Chichén Itzá in the Yucatán Peninsula has a sculpture of the head of Kukulkan, the Feathered Serpent, at the bottom corner of its pyramid. The Maya architects aligned the pyramid with the sun. At the fall and spring equinoxes, a shadow strikes that corner of the pyramid, making it appear as if the serpent is slithering down the pyramid.

Chaac, the Rain God (Chac, Chak, Chaahk)

Chaac was the god of storms, rain, and fertility (because his rain enabled plants to grow). He was another ancient god worshiped in Teotihuacan by at least the first century CE, where he was paired with the Feathered Serpent. His name was Tlaloc in the Nahuatl language; the Zapotecs called him Cocijo, and the Totonac called him Tajin.

Chaac is easily recognized by his facial features. He always had fangs, usually two long fangs extending downward from each side of his upper jaw. He frequently had round, googly eyes, and the Maya often pictured him with a long, droopy nose, something like the tapirs of the rainforest. He had large ear ornaments of shell. Many of his sculptures only show his head, but his body is sometimes pictured as a human with scales like a reptile.

Chaac, the Maya rain god"

Chaac was an individual god, but he also had four manifestations called Chaacs. They represented North, East, South, and West, and the colors red, yellow, white, and black. In the Yucatán Peninsula, four priests called Chaacs held the arms and legs of a sacrificial victim.

In addition to rain, Chaac was the god of cenotes, springs, streams, and wells. What's a *cenote*? It's a natural well or sinkhole and played a key role in rituals honoring Chaac.

The upper part of the Yucatán Peninsula has no rivers. The few lakes are too salty for drinking water or for crops. However, the cenotes throughout the region give access to fresh water from the underground aquifer.

One of the cenotes in Chichén Itzá was sacred to the Maya. They threw children, gold, and jade into it as offerings to Chaac. Researchers recently conducted DNA analysis of the skeletons of sixty-four victims in an underground chamber near the cenote. They discovered they were all little boys under six years old. Many were close relatives, including two sets of twins, buried there between 800 and 1,000 CE.

In Maya mythology, Chaac's brother was K'inich Ahau, the sun god. In one myth, the brothers had cruel adoptive parents. Through deception and battle, they defeated the evil pair and freed themselves. However, Chaac later stole his brother's wife and was punished for his sin. His tears of agony and repentance became the rain.

K'inich Ahau, the Sun God
(Kinich Ahau, Kinich Ajaw, "God G")

K'inich Ahau was the face of the sun and a god of medicine and healing. His wife was Ixazalvoh, the goddess of childbirth, female sexuality, healing, life, water, and weaving. Paintings show K'inich Ahau as a middle-aged man with a hooked nose and huge square eyes that are crossed. Like his brother, Chaac, he had fangs at the corners of his mouth. K'inich Ahau was a form of the creator god Itzamná. He was the god of the eastern sea paradise, where he became a mythical water bird or a young man paddling a canoe. The Maya believed that when the sun set in the west, K'inich Ahau passed into the underworld as the "Night Sun" or "Jaguar God of the Underworld." He went through the underworld and came out again on the eastern horizon at sunrise.

K'inich Ahau, the sun god⁹

Itzamná, Supreme God of the Sky and Wisdom

Itzamná was the chief god of the Maya, the founder of their culture. He was an "upper god," ruling from the sky. He taught the Maya how to write and how to grow corn. He introduced them to the calendar, medicine, art, and architecture. He was a creator and healer with the power to raise the dead. Paintings and sculptures show him as an elderly, large-nosed man. Other times, he has the features of a caiman (an alligator-like reptile). Another portrayal is the Bird of Heaven (Itzam Yeh), holding a two-headed snake and sitting on the World Tree (Ceiba). Itzamná's wife was Ixchel, the moon goddess.

Sometimes, Itzamná is referred to as a mortal, the prophet Zamná, who brought the books of learning to Chichén Itzá. He is equated with the tenth-century CE Toltec king, Topiltzin Quetzalcoatl, who, according to legend, crossed the Gulf of Mexico to the Yucatán Peninsula. In Toltec accounts, Topiltzin was a wise king who worshiped Quetzalcoatl, the Feathered Serpent, and forbade human sacrifice. Yet, he was forced out of his city of Tula in central Mexico. Archaeological evidence shows that the Toltecs did colonize the Yucatán Peninsula and built part of Chichén Itzá. The city was a blend of Maya and Toltec architecture. However, the Toltecs did *not* introduce writing to the Maya. The Maya wrote with sophisticated hieroglyphics a thousand years before the Toltec culture emerged.

Itzamná, supreme god of the Maya[10]

One manifestation of Itzamná is a blue dragon or caiman. A painting in the *Dresden Codex* shows Itzamná's head protruding out of the gaping mouth of a huge reptile. The *Dresden Codex* is a book written by the Maya in the eleventh or twelfth century about astronomy, Maya mythology, and medicine. The "amate" paper of the precious document was made from pounded *Ficus* bark. It folds up like an accordion but stretches to about twelve feet when unfolded. The pages are covered with Maya hieroglyphics and brilliant paintings of many of their deities. Immediately above and below the blue reptile are bars and dots, representing the Maya number system. Above the numbers are two rows of small pictures, which are glyphs, the Maya writing form.

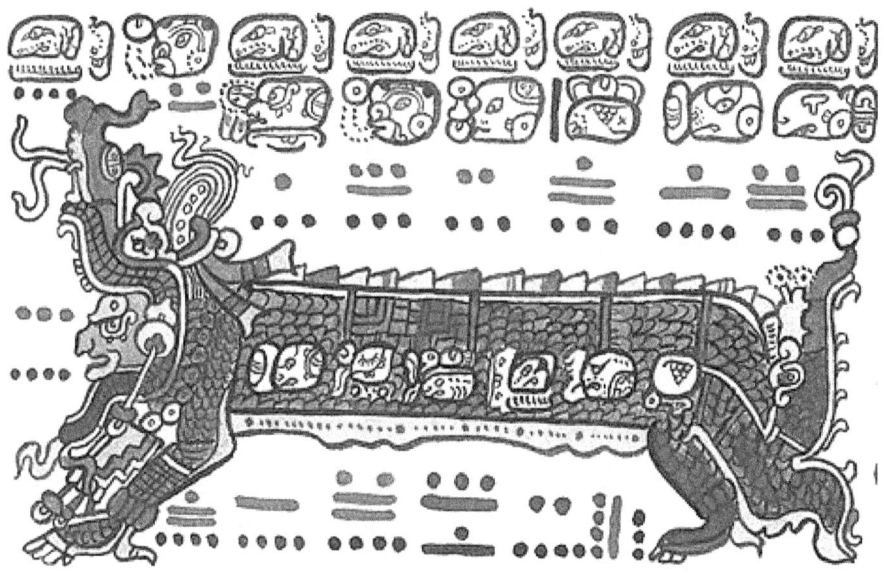

Itzamná's manifestation as a blue caiman[11]

Ixchel, Rainbow Goddess of the Moon (Ix Chel)

Ixchel, which means "Lady Rainbow," was Itzamná's wife and the jaguar goddess. She juggled multiple roles. As a war goddess, she is pictured with claws and surrounded by bones. She assisted with rain and farming. Maya doctors consulted with Ixchel on medical matters. Ladies who wanted to get pregnant prayed to her, as she was the goddess of conception. She was so successful in that area that she and Itzamná had thirteen sons. Some myths said they were the parents of all the younger gods. Four of her sons, the Bacabs, had the job of holding up the four corners of the sky.

Most importantly, Ixchel was the goddess of the moon and of change, governing the tides and menstrual cycles. One might think "Lady Rainbow," the moon goddess, would be a gleaming beauty. However, the Maya portrayed her as a murderous old lady with a rattlesnake coiled on her head. Sometimes, she had fangs and wore skulls as decoration. However, she was the goddess of change, so she could transform herself into a delicate young woman as needed.

Ixchel, the moon goddess[12]

The Maya made pilgrimages to the island of Cozumel, just off the Yucatán Peninsula, to pray at her shrine. Cozumel held so many shrines and statues of Maya goddesses that the Spanish commander Cortés named it "Isla Mujeres" or "Island of Women." Even after the Maya converted to Catholicism, they continued praying to Ixchel, sometimes as the Virgin Mary.

Yum Kaax, God of Nature (Yum Caax)

Yum Kaax, whose name meant "Lord of the Wild," was the protector and sustainer of the environment. Maya artwork shows Yum Kaax as youthful and handsome. He was among the youngest gods and a son of Itzamná and Ixchel. He guarded the woodlands and wild animals. He also cared for the cacao trees, the Maya's precious source of chocolate. Moreover, he was the patron of hunters. That might seem paradoxical since he was supposed to protect the wild animals. Yet, removing a few of the animals for human food prevented overpopulation and lack of food for the animals. The Maya considered him a kind protector of humans, wildlife, and the jungles.

Yum Kaax, god of nature[18]

Before going hunting, the Maya men prayed to Yum Kaax, asking for his permission to kill and for his protection. He could help a hunter's arrow find its mark. However, if the hunter failed to show proper reverence, Yum Kaax could cause the arrow to veer off and miss. If people carelessly harmed the environment or if hunters were cruel to the animals, the wrath of Yum Kaax would fall on them.

Buluc Chabtan, God of War and Violence (God F)

The Maya regularly sacrificed humans to this "bad" god who brought violence, war, and sudden death. He was known for capriciously setting houses on fire and randomly murdering people by stabbing them. Illustrations of this fierce god show him roasting people over a fire or covered with maggots. He often has a wavy black line on the left side of his red face, swirling from his eyebrow to his jawline. He is sometimes pictured with Ah Puch, the primary lord of death.

Buluc-Chabtan, god of war[14]

The Death Gods, Lords of Xibalba

The Maya called their underworld "*Xibalba.*" It was the "Place of Fright" ruled by **Ah Puch (One Death), Seven Death, Flying Scab, Gathered Blood,** and several other gods. Owls, jaguars, and dogs represented these gods. One Death and Seven Death caused blood diseases.

Ah Puch (Cizin), whose name meant "Yellow Pus Demon," had a good side and a bad side. On the one hand, he generated darkness, disaster, earthquakes, and death. He loved to roam about, uprooting the trees planted by the rain god, Chaac. He would swell people up until pus oozed from their legs and their faces turned yellow with jaundice. However, Ah Puch was also the god of new beginnings or regeneration through childbirth.

One myth about Cizin (the "Smelly One") in southern Guatemala is that when a dead soul entered the underworld, the god burned the person's mouth and bottom. If the soul cried out, he poured ice-cold water over them. Usually, this caused the poor soul to screech in shock, and then Cizin would burn them up completely. If the souls were fortunate, another god, **Sucunyum**, intervened. He cleaned the soul with spit and set it free to roam wherever it wanted. Maya artwork sometimes shows Cizin as a dancing skeleton smoking a cigarette. He also wears a "death collar" of eyeballs. Other times, he appears as a reptile.

Two lesser gods of Xibalba were *Sweeping Demon* and *Stabbing Demon*. Their job was to stab people who didn't properly sweep around their houses or take the trash out. Some guardians of the Maya underworld were the bat demons called **Camazotz**. They lived in the deepest depth of Xibalba, where the only sound in the frigid darkness was the eerie screeching of bats. The Camazotz's job was to eat the heads of anyone who entered their domain. They had human bodies with bat wings and a bat head with long fangs.

Camazotz, a bat demon[15]

Roundup Activity: Who Am I?

Choose the correct answer for each description from the list below. Check your answers in the back of the book.

1. I was a creator god who taught the humans about writing, medicine, and law. _____

2. I was the droopy-nosed, fanged rain god. _____

3. I was the face of the sun and the god of healing. _____

4. I was the supreme god of the sky. _____

5. I was the moon goddess and wife of Itzamná. _____

6. I was Ixchel's son and god of nature. _____

7. I was the bad god of violence and war. _____

8. I ruled Xibalba, the underworld. _____

9. We were bat demons who ate people's heads _____

10. We stabbed people who didn't take out the trash or keep their yards clean.

Chapter 3: The Hero Twins and the Underworld

This chapter dives into the adventurous tale of the Hero Twins, Hunahpu and Xbalanque. Their perilous journey through Xibalba is a pivotal part of the *Popol Vuh*. It highlights ingenuity, courage, and the triumph of good over evil. As this story unfolds, remember that it is told in the present tense in the *Popol Vuh*. In the Maya storytelling style, the gathered listeners could imagine the events happening at that moment.

Who Was the Twins' Father?

The first two gods, Grandmother Xmucane and Grandfather Xpiyacoc, had twin sons: One (Hun) Hunahpu and Seven (Vucub) Hunahpu. One Hunahpu married the heron goddess Xbaquiyalo, and they had two sons called the "Monkey Twins": One Batz and One Chouen. These boys weren't the same as the Hero Twins, who were born later from the same father but a different mother. The Monkey Twins' mother died young. Remember, Maya gods weren't immortal. Here's the first part of the story.

| Hun Hunahpu Ballplayer | Xbaquiyalo Heron Goddess | Vucub Hunahpu Ballplayer |

One Hunahpu, Xbaquiyalo, and Seven Hunahpu[16]

Hunahpu and Seven Hunahpu are good, wise men. They teach One Hunahpu's sons to be jade workers, metalsmiths, and sculptors. The two older men and the two boys love to play ball together. They play the ball game every day.

What Was Pok Ta' Pok, the Maya Ball Game?

The Maya and the rest of Mesoamerica had a game they played with a rubber ball. They played for fun, but the game also had religious significance. By at least 1700 BCE, the Olmec people had invented rubber by mixing the sap of the rubber tree and morning glory vines. They used this to make balls. Of course, the balls weren't filled with air like they are today. They were solid rubber, so they were quite heavy—around eight pounds. Thus, the ballplayers wore helmets and padding.

The Maya played their ball game in a sunken court with rings on the wall for goals. The game was a little like volleyball in that the ball couldn't hit the ground. However, the players weren't allowed to use their hands. They used their right knee, right hip, and right elbow to keep the ball in the air, going in the right direction and, hopefully, through one of the rings.

Goal ring at Chichén Itzá ball court[17]

Archaeologists working in southern Mexico's Maya city of Toniná believe they have found evidence that the Maya mixed cremated ashes, possibly of their rulers, with the rubber when making the balls. They found a crypt below a pyramid dating to the mid-700s CE that had about four hundred jars, some holding ashes and others holding sap from the morning glory vine and rubber tree.

They also found nearby sculptures of people *inside* rubber balls. The Maya did use human remains in other sacred rituals. However, more testing must be done to prove that the Maya mixed human ashes into their rubber balls. The Maya ball game was an essential part of religious festivals and usually accompanied by human sacrifice, perhaps of the losing captain. Maybe the ashes were from the sacrificial victims.

Now, let's pick back up with the story.

Figurine of a Maya ball player with protective padding (600 to 950 CE)[18]

One Hunahpu and Seven Hunahpu Irritate the Lords of Xibalba

One Hunahpu, his sons, and his brother make so much noise playing the ball game that they wake up the lords of Xibalba (the "Lords of Death").

"What's going on up there on the Earth's surface? What's all that stomping and shouting? They're disrespecting us with all this noise over our heads! Let's summon those arrogant gods down here. We'll play ball with them and defeat them! And then, we'll take all their equipment—their helmets, arm protectors, and face guards."

So, One Death and Seven Death call their messengers, the owls. "Go up to the Earth's surface and command One Hunahpu and Seven Hunahpu to come down to Xibalba to play ball."

The owls fly up to the Earth's surface and deliver the message.

"Okay," the brothers answer. "But first, we need to go see our mother."

Their father, Xpiyacoc, has died, but their mother, Xmucane, is still alive. One Hunahpu leaves his ball with their mother. "The Lords of Death have summoned us to Xibalba. We have to go."

He tells his sons, the Monkey Twins, "Stay here with your grandmother. Sing and play the flute to warm her heart while we're gone. And don't forget to keep up with your writing and carving!"

As Xmucane weeps, her sons comfort her. "Don't worry, Mother! We won't die. Don't cry."

One Hunahpu and Seven Hunahpu in Xibalba

Guided by the owls, One Hunahpu and Seven Hunahpu descend into Xibalba, walking down steep steps until they come to Trembling Canyon and Murmuring Canyon. They wade through Scorpion River but are not stung. Then they cross Blood River but are fine because they don't drink from it. The third river is Pus River, but they cross it uneventfully. Finally, they come to a crossroads, which the Maya believed was especially dangerous because each direction had special powers. At the crossroads, they have the choice of Red Road (east), Black Road (west), Yellow Road (south), and White Road (north).

"Take me! I'm the lords' road," calls the Black Road.

The Black Road takes them to their destination but also leads them to their defeat as the sun sets in the west. When they arrive at the hall of the Lords of Death, the gods are all seated.

The brothers politely greet them. "Good morning, Flying Scab. Good morning, Gathered Blood."

Flying Scab and Gathered Blood reply, "We're glad you're here. Tomorrow, you'll put on your protective gear for the ball game. Come! Sit down with us."

It's a trick. When the brothers sit down, the bench is a burning hot rock that scorches their bottoms. The Lords of Death laugh so hard their stomachs hurt and they can't catch their breath.

"Just go up to the house," the gods tell the brothers. "Someone will give you a torch and some cigars to enjoy."

The Lords of Death plot their evil scheme as soon as the brothers leave. "Tomorrow, we sacrifice them! One little mistake, and they will die because of how we play ball!" they gloat. The ball they play with isn't an ordinary rubber ball. They call it "White Dagger" because sharp, jagged ends of broken bones stick out of the ball.

Meanwhile, the brothers get to the House of Darkness. A servant brings the torch and some cigars. "Don't burn up the torch or the cigars. You must return them to the Lords of Death in the morning, intact."

However, the brothers smoke each cigar, leaving nothing. Their torch also burns out. They discover they can't sleep in the House of Darkness. They must now travel through several other houses. They hike to Shivering House, which is covered with frost. A howling, icy wind blows through the house. Next is Jaguar House, where jaguars growl and gnash their teeth. The fourth place is Bat House, where shrieking bats fly all around. The fifth house is Blade House, full of clattering, clashing knife blades.

After a night of trials, the brothers emerge from Blade House, where Flying Scab and Gathered Blood await them.

"Where's the cigars and torch you got last night?" the Lords of Death ask.

"We finished them off, O Lords," the brothers answer.

"In that case, you must die."

The Lords of Death sacrifice One Hunahpu and Seven Hunahpu and bury them under the Crushing Ball Court. Before burying One Hunahpu, they cut off his head. "Put it in that tree by the road," the lords command.

When his head is set in the calabash tree, it produces fruit, which it has never done before. So many gourds grow in the tree that they cover One Hunahpu's face. Everyone in Xibalba comes to see the remarkable sight. "We should never eat this fruit or sit under this tree," they whisper.

Possible sculpture of One Hunahpu's head in the calabash tree[19]

A Princess Conceives

Scattered Blood's daughter hears about the tree and can't wait to see it. "The fruit looks so delicious. I don't think it will hurt me. No one will know if I take some."

Hunahpu's voice startles her. "You really don't want this fruit."

"Oh, but I do!" says Xquic (Blood Moon), the plucky princess.

"All right, stick out your hand."

The princess reaches her hand toward the skull, and One Hunahpu spits on her.

"My skull is no longer functional, but my saliva is my essence. I will continue on in my sons."

Princess Blood Moon returns home, pregnant from the saliva. When she is six months pregnant, her father, Gathered Blood, notices her condition. He calls a council with the other Lords of Death.

"My daughter is pregnant with a bastard!" he growls.

"Find out who the father is," the lords recommend. "Dig the truth out. If she doesn't tell, she must be sacrificed."

So, Gathered Blood questions Princess Xquic. "Who is responsible for the child you're carrying?"

"What child?" asks the princess. "I haven't been with a man."

"Of course you have! You're promiscuous!"

He turns to the four owls, "Sacrifice her! Bring her heart back to me in a bowl so I can show the other lords."

The owls lift the princess with their talons and fly away.

Princess Xquic tells the owls, "The baby in my womb is not from sin but from a special creation. It's because I admired the skull of One Hunahpu at the Crushing Ball Court. Please don't sacrifice me, messenger owls."

The owls feel compassion. "We don't want you to die. Yet, your father told us to bring back your heart. What will we put in this bowl?"

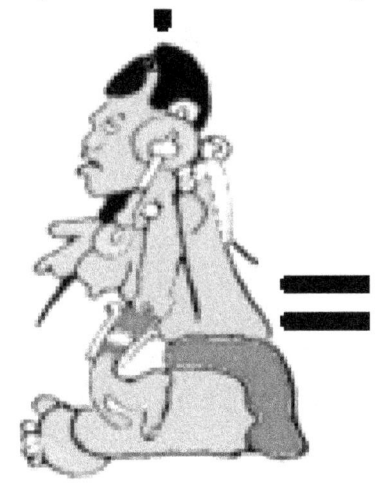

Xquic
Infernal Goddess

Princess Xquic, daughter of Gathered Blood[20]

"Take the red sap of the Dragon's Blood tree," says the princess.

As the red sap fills the bowl, looking like blood, some of it congeals. It forms a small round ball that looks like a heart.

"You will be highly respected on earth for this deed of kindness," the princess promises them.

"Very well, maiden. We will keep you safe. First, we must take this substitute heart to the Lords of Death."

The owls fly back to the Lords of Death.

"Did you succeed?"

"Yes, lords. Here is her heart in the bottom of this bowl of blood."

Flying Scab takes the bowl and lifts the "heart" as the bright red sap drips from his fingers. "Stir up the coals and place this bowl over it!" he commands.

So, they fan the coals in the firepit until they flame up. As the congealed sap bubbles in the bowl, it emits a delicious fragrance. The gods lean over to savor the scent. Meanwhile, the owls quickly sneak the princess to the Earth's surface.

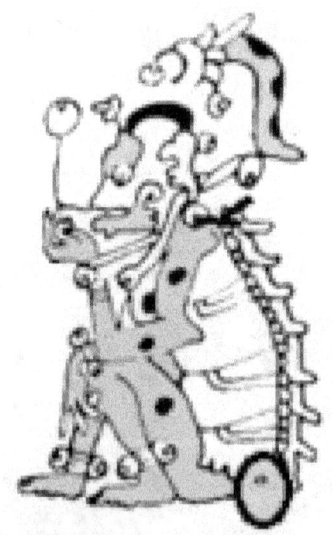

Cuchumaquic
Lord of Xibalba

Gathered Blood[11]

The Princess and the Maize Miracle

After escaping Xibalba, Princess Xquic hurries to the cottage of the creator goddess Xmucane, One Hunahpu's mother. "My lady, I am your daughter-in-law."

"Are my sons still alive?" Xmucane asks anxiously.

The ancient goddess begins weeping as she realizes the truth. She looks at Xquic's swollen belly. "I think you should go back from where you came."

"My lady, these twins inside me are your grandsons. You will see One Hunahpu's face on their faces when they are born."

One Hunahpu's older sons, the Monkey Twins, comfort their grandmother, yet Xmucane glares at Xquic. "I don't want you here. You're not truly my daughter-in-law. You weren't married to my son. You're only pregnant through immorality. My sons are dead!"

"But these babies are the sons of One Hunahpu!" Xquic insists.

"Alright, then. If you're really my daughter-in-law, go get some food to feed my grandsons." She hands Xquic an enormous net. "Fill this net with corn and bring it back!"

Xquic traipses out to the cornfield, but she only finds one cornstalk, which only has one ear of corn. Her heart sinks. "Where will I find enough corn to fill my net?"

Xquic pulls on the corn silk sticking out of the one ear of corn. As she pulls, multiple ears of corn come out of the ear, and she fills her net. The animals carry the overflowing net for her as she returns to Xmucane.

Xmucane looks suspiciously at all the corn. "Where did you get all this? Did you steal it?"

The old goddess marches to the maize field and inspects the lone corn stalk. She sees the ear of corn still on it. She sees marks in the earth where the heavy net had rested on the soil. Xmucane rushes home. "Now I know you're truly my daughter-in-law! My grandsons in your belly already have superpowers!"

The Hero Twins, Hunahpu and Xbalanque[22]

The Hero Twins Are Summoned to the Underworld

After the twin boys are born, Xquic names them Hunahpu and Xbalanque. As teens, they discover their father's old ball court and begin playing ball. Yet again, their noise aggravates the gods underneath in Xibalba.

"Who's up there now, stomping about? Call them down here!" the Lords of Death order the messenger owls. "Tell them they must play a ball game with us in seven days."

The owls fly to Grandmother Xmucane's house, but the twins are out on the ball court, playing ball. The owls tell Xmucane, "The boys must come to Xibalba in seven days to play ball with the Lords of Death."

When the owls fly away, Xmucane weeps bitterly, remembering what happened to her sons in Xibalba. Just then, she feels itchy and realizes a louse is in her hair. She pulls him out and sends him to tell her grandsons about the summons from Xibalba. As the louse scuttles toward the ball court, he meets a toad.

"Where are you going?" asks the toad.

"I'm taking a message to the twin boys."

"It will take you all day at this rate," says the toad. "Let me swallow you, and we'll get there faster."

"Well, okay," says the louse. The toad swallows him and hops toward the ball court. But then, a snake slithers out on the path.

"Where are you going, toad?"

"I'm carrying a message in my belly to the twin boys at the ball court."

"You're not moving very fast," observes the snake. "If I swallow you, maybe we'll get there faster."

The snake swallows the toad and quickly crawls toward the ball court. Just then, a falcon swoops down from the sky, grabs the snake, and eats it. He flies to the ball court and lands next to it. When the boys see him, they grab their blowguns and shoot the falcon, hitting him in the eye.

The falcon calls out, "I have a message for you in my belly. But first, you must heal my eye."

The boys cut a thin slice of rubber off their ball and put it on the falcon's eye, which heals it. From then on, the laughing falcon has a black patch on his eye. The falcon vomits up the snake, which vomits up the toad. But when the toad tries to vomit the louse, he can't. The twins pry his mouth open and find the louse clinging to the top of the toad's mouth.

"What is your message?" the boys ask.

"Your grandmother sent me to tell you that in seven days, you must go to Xibalba to play ball with the Lords of Death. You must take all your equipment—your ball, neck yoke, arm protectors, and padding."

The boys hurry to their grandmother's cottage and plant two ears of corn in the floor. "Grandmother, if these ears of corn dry up, you'll know we're dead. But if they sprout, that's a sign that we're alive."

Journey to Xibalba

The boys take their blowguns and descend into the underworld. They must pass through the same trials their father faced, yet their mother is a princess of Xibalba. They know what to expect. They call a mosquito to help them. "Go ahead of us and bite each of the Lords of Death."

So, the mosquito flies to the hall where the Lords of Death are gathered. He bites each god in turn.

"Ow!" screams a god.

"What is it, One Death?"

"Something bit me!"

Another god yelps.

"What's the matter, Flying Scab?"

"Something just stung me."

As the mosquito bites each god, they call out, and the others speak their name, asking what's wrong. This way, the mosquito learns the names of the Lords of Death: One Death, Seven Death, Flying Scab, Gathered Blood, Pus Demon, Jaundice Demon, Bone Staff, Skull Staff, Pack Strap, Bloody Teeth, and Bloody Claws.

When Hunahpu and Xbalanque walk in, a demon commands them to greet the Lords of Death. The twins greet each god with the correct name. When the gods invite them to sit on the bench, they refuse. "That's a heated stone!"

The gods send them to the House of Darkness, but when the messenger hands them cigars and a torch, they do not light them. The next morning, they hand the untouched cigars and torch to the Lords of Death.

"How did they do this? Who are their parents?" wonder the Lords of Death.

The Ball Game in Xibalba

"Let's play ball!" say the gods. "We'll use ours."

"No, we'll play with our rubber ball," the twins insist. "Your ball's a skull."

"It's not really a skull. It's just a painting of a skull on a rubber ball."

"No, that's a real skull!"

"We promise! It isn't a skull."

"Oh, all right!" says Hunahpu.

One of the lords throws the ball toward Hunahpu. But this is the "White Dagger" ball, with sharp, jagged bones sticking out. It thrashes around as the boys jump out of the way.

"You're trying to kill us!" the boys cry out. "We came when you called us. Now, we'll leave!"

"Oh, please don't go! We can play with your ball," the lords urge. The boys stay, but now the teams must decide on the prize for the winners.

"How about four bowls of flowers?" ask the lords.

"Sounds fine," say the boys.

The first round of the ball game begins, and both sides have equal skill. Yet, the boys are outnumbered and must play harder with no other teammates. Finally, the exhausted twins admit defeat.

"Bring us our flowers in the morning. We'll play the next round then," the lords say.

Maya ball game carving[23]

The boys have to stay in the Blade House that night, which would have cut them into pieces. However, the boys use their powers of enchantment, and the blades lower. The boys then order the ants to go cut the flowers for the gods' prize. The ants march out to the gardens of One Death and Seven Death.

The gods had already warned their whippoorwill guardsmen, "Don't go to sleep tonight. Stay alert and look out for the twins. They're going to try to take flowers for tomorrow's prize."

The birds fly around the garden, keeping an eye out for the boys. However, they don't notice the swarm of ants marching through the garden and cutting the flowers. The following morning, the boys arrive at the ball court carrying four bowls of flowers. The faces of the Lords of Death pale. The boys have gotten the best of them.

The two teams are evenly matched this time, with no clear winner. "We'll meet again at dawn tomorrow," announce the lords.

On this night, the boys stay in Shivering House. A howling icy wind blows through the rooms, covering them with hail. Yet, the twins use their superpowers to melt the ice and stay warm. When they show up for the next morning's game, the Lords of Death almost collapse in astonishment. "What? They didn't die? They should be frozen solid!"

Once again, the game is a draw, so they agree to meet the next day. That night, Hunahpu and Xbalanque stay in Jaguar House. "Don't eat us!" the twins command the jaguars. "We'll give you food."

The boys give bones to the jaguars to eat. After a while, the night watchman peeks in the window and sees the jaguars chewing on the bones. "They must have killed the boys and are gnawing on their bones now."

The lords' jaws drop when the twins come out of Jaguar House at dawn, safe and sound. "What kind of people are they?" they wonder.

The boys stay in the House of Fire the next night but emerge safe and sound the following day, with nothing singed. That night, they sleep in the Bat House. These bats are enormous Camazotz demons with snouts like a knife blade. The boys crawl inside their blowguns so the bats can't get to them. After some time, the bats are quiet, and Hunahpu wonders if it's dawn yet. He sticks his head out of his blowgun, and a bat slices it off with his snout.

"Is it morning yet?" asks Xbalanque. But Hunahpu doesn't answer. Xbalanque only hears the rustling bats.

The bat carries Hunahpu's head to the Lords of Death, who put it at the top of the ball court. Meanwhile, in the dark before dawn, Xbalanque calls the woodland animals to his aid. A coati brings him a round squash, which Xbalanque carves into the head of his brother. The creator god, Hurricane, comes down to the Bat House to help Xbalanque with the squash head. By dawn, the head can speak.

"Don't try to play ball," Xbalanque warns his brother. "Just keep your squash head on."

They go together to the ball court and shock the Lords of Death. Hunahpu's head is on his shoulders but also on top of the ball court.

The ball game starts, and the lords send it down the court to Xbalanque. He knocks it out of the court and into the tomato patch, and a rabbit hops out. The Lords of Death run after the rabbit, and while they are distracted, the twins get Hunahpu's real head back.

Once Hunahpu's actual head is back on his shoulders, they call out to the lords, "We found the ball!"

But the ball is the round squash head. The two teams play fiercely until Xbalanque strikes the round squash, which breaks open and spews seeds everywhere. Thus, Hunahpu and Xbalanque defeat the Lords of Death.

Roundup Activity: When Did It Happen?

Number the following events in order based on when they happened in the story. Check your answers in the back of the book.

( ) A bat cuts off Hunahpu's head.

( ) A mosquito helps the Hero Twins, Hunahpu and Xbalanque, in Xibalba.

( ) Hunahpu and Xbalanque defeat the Lords of Death.

( ) One Hunahpu and Seven Hunahpu sit on a burning hot rock that scorches their bottoms.

( ) One Hunahpu's wife, Xbaquiyalo, gives birth to the Monkey Twins.

( ) Princess Xquic gets pregnant from One Hunahpu's spit.

( ) The Hero Twins discover their father's old ball court.

( ) The Hero Twins lose the first round of the ball game.

( ) The Lords of Death command One Hunahpu and Seven Hunahpu to play ball in Xibalba.

( ) The Lords of Death sacrifice One Hunahpu and Seven Hunahpu.

( ) The owls help Xquic escape from being sacrificed.

( ) Xbalanque replaces Hunahpu's head with a round squash.

Chapter 4: Unlocking the Maya Calendar

Like us, the Maya used a calendar to measure time, remember important dates, and celebrate festivals. Yet, it was more complicated for the Maya (and most Mesoamerican cultures) because they had one calendar for the solar year and a shorter calendar for religious festivals. Astronomy and timekeeping played vital roles in Maya religion, and their mythology swirled around the celestial bodies. They even aligned the ceremonial buildings in their cities to face the sunrise or sunset on pivotal dates. According to their mythology, Itzamná, the supreme god of wisdom, introduced the calendar system to the Maya.

What Were the Tzolk'in and the Haab'?

The *Tzolk'in* was the Maya religious festival calendar. It was only 260 days with twenty "months," each thirteen days long. The *Haab'* followed the 365-day solar year. As we know, the solar year is actually 365.242 days. That's why we have a "leap year" every four years to keep the calendar on point. However, the Maya didn't have a leap year. Their 365-day year is called a "vague" solar calendar because it eventually drifts away from what the sun is doing. It would take 1,510 years to get back on track.

Oddly, in the solar calendar (Haab'), the Maya months didn't follow the thirty-day lunar month. Instead, months had twenty days, like the festival calendar. That gave them eighteen months with five days left over, so they had one really short month. That five-day month, called **Wayeb**, was a dangerous time when the barriers between Earth and the underworld dissolved. Evil spirits rose from Xibalba to create havoc. Most people stayed inside and avoided washing their hair during those five days so they wouldn't be susceptible to the demons.

Why twenty days in the religious and solar calendar months? The Maya counted by twenties instead of tens. By contrast, we measure years by decades and use the decimal system of tens for money. The Egyptians used the "tens" system by 3000 BCE, probably because one can count to ten using fingers. The Maya apparently counted their fingers *and* toes in their "twenties" system. What about the thirteen days in the Maya festival months? The Maya had thirteen levels of the upperworld, the home of the gods.

The Maya kept track of their calendar system with their hieroglyphics, representing numbers using dots and bars. For numbers one through four, they used one to four dots. They wrote the number five as a bar. Six through nine were a bar and one to four dots. Ten was two bars. One dot and a shell represented twenty. Two dots and a shell represented forty.

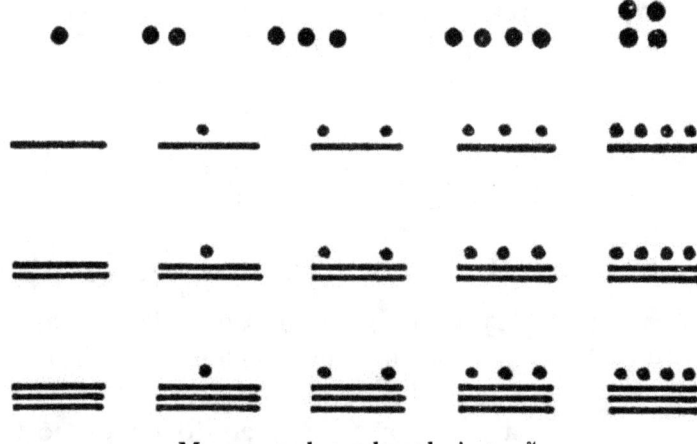

Maya numerals one through nineteen[24]

The Maya Calendar Round: Coordinating Two Calendars

The Maya had the complex task of coordinating their solar calendar (Haab') and festival calendar (Tzolk'in). Their "Calendar Round" was the instrument they used to keep track. It had four interlocking circles.

The largest outside circle represented Haab'. A small picture or glyph stood for each of the nineteen months. For instance, the month "Sotz" had a pictogram of a monkey's head.

The next circle had the numbers one through twenty, using the system of dots, bars, and a shell. Inside that was the third circle with twenty glyphs representing the twenty months of Tzolk'in, the festival year. For instance, the month "Ok" had a pictogram of a dog's head. The innermost circle had dots and bars representing the thirteen days of each festival month.

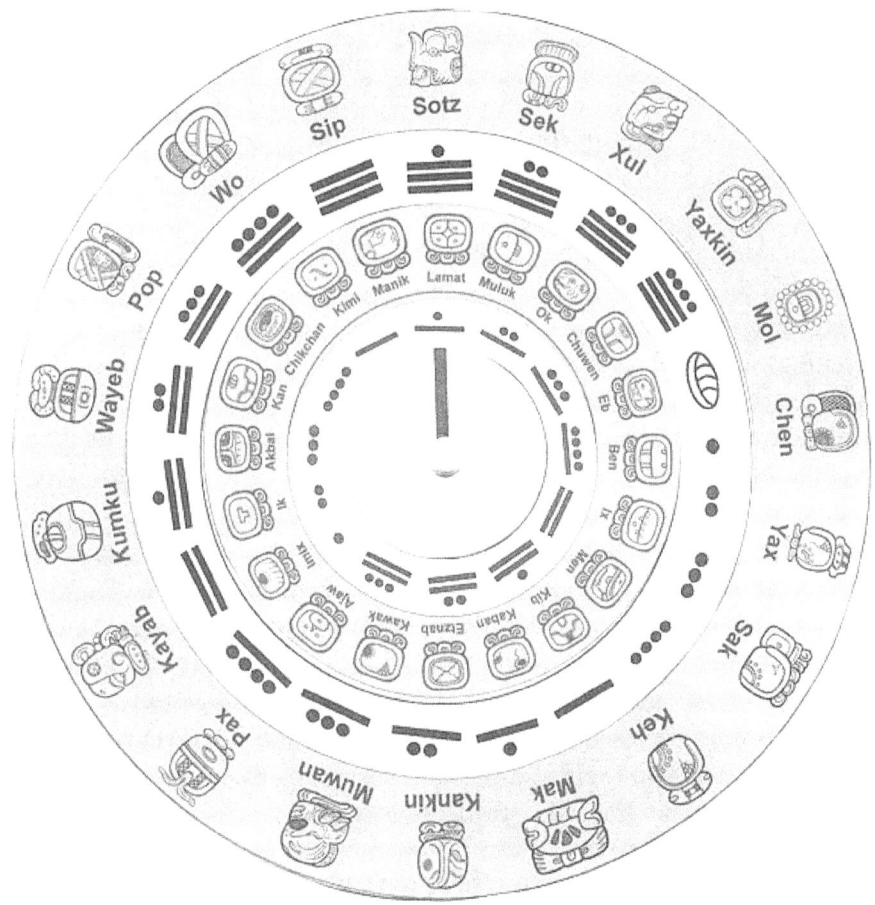

Maya Calendar Round[35]

The Calendar Round enabled the Maya to keep track of the days of both the solar year and the festival year. Basically, the Tzolk'in festival year was a wheel within the wheel of the solar Haab' year. The local "day keeper"—a shaman or astrologer—used four pebbles or kernels of corn on the Calendar Round to mark time in the festival and solar years. It took fifty-two years for the same two dates on the festival and solar cycles to occur together again. Thus, that day was paramount. It marked a new fifty-two-year "cycle" of life.

How Did the Maya Track History with the Long Count Calendar?

The Maya perceived time in cycles rather than linear or along a straight line. However, they needed a way to mark key dates in the past (or future), such as creation, the reign of an important king, or solar eclipses. For that, they used the Long Count calendar, which measures time in five cycles. They thought the gods had completed creation precisely on August 11, 3114 BCE. Intriguingly, that date is close to when the Pre-Olmec civilization emerged in Tabasco and Veracruz, near southern Mexico's Gulf Coast. The Olmec passed on a cultural legacy to the Maya.

We count history in weeks, months, decades, centuries, and millennia. The Maya mostly measured shorter blocks of time in multiples of twenty. Twenty days was a *winal*, the Maya month. Eighteen winals, or 360 days, was a *tun*, the rough equivalent of the Maya year. Twenty tuns, or 7,200 days (almost twenty years), was a *k'atun*. Twenty k'atuns, or 144,00 days (395 years), was a *b ak tun*.

The Maya counted long-term history in 5,128-year cycles. Starting from creation (3114 BCE), they thought the first cycle of time would end in 2012 CE. That did *not* mean they thought the world would *end* on that date, as many misguided media outlets falsely screeched. The Maya thought 2012 CE was when a new Long Count cycle would begin, just like the shorter cycles began every fifty-two years. The Maya used the Long Count dates on their monuments, recording their kings' birth dates and deaths and what they did during their reigns.

What Was the Significance of Astronomy?

The Maya were stargazers, and their observations of the night skies informed them that the universe was orderly. They tracked the cycles of the visible planets, especially Venus, but also Mars, Jupiter, and Saturn. They noted the movement of constellations. They could predict celestial events, such as the cycles of Venus and lunar and solar eclipses. They figured out that five Venus cycles roughly equaled eight years.

The Maya believed that the planets and stars represented gods and that the universe included both spiritual and tangible elements. For instance, they believed the Milky Way re-enacted creation as it passed through its cycles. On the evenings of August 13 and February 5, the Milky Way forms a north-south axis. On these dates, the Maya believed the Milky Way represented the "world tree" that linked the Earth with heaven. They thought this was the tree that Seven Macaw sat in after the great flood when he bragged of being the new sun. As the Milky Way began tilting toward the horizon, the Maya thought the dark rift was a celestial crocodile. In some *Chilam Balam* versions of the Maya creation myth, Itzam Cab Ain was a caiman or crocodile that formed the new Earth.

The maize god and Itzamná discuss how to create humans.[36]

Finally, the Milky Way reaches its east-west axis and transforms into the maize god in a canoe. In a version of the Maya creation myth, after the Hero Twins defeat the Lords of Xibalba, their father, One Hunahpu, becomes the maize god. He was the one who suggested to the other gods that they make corn dough to form humans after their first two failed attempts with mud and wood.

How Did the Maya Track Celestial Bodies?

Although they didn't have telescopes, the Maya used simple tools, like cords, sticks, and viewing tubes, to observe the stars, moon, and planets. One of these tools was a "cross stick." It was simply a long stick stuck in the ground at a right angle. They used the shadow cast by the stick to know when it was high noon and to predict when the solstices and equinoxes would happen. A straight line traveling north and south, called a "meridian device," tracked the stars and planets as they crossed from north to south. The Maya carefully observed the horizon to determine when celestial bodies rose and set over time.

The Maya built structures to aid their observations of the night sky. For instance, they had viewing platforms in several cities. They also built more sophisticated astronomical observation structures with viewing windows lined up with specific celestial events. El Caracol ("The Observatory") at Chichén Itzá has a round tower with a domed roof and windows perfectly aligned to see the cycles of Venus. A doorway at the Governor's Palace at Uxmal aligned with Venus' setting as the evening star.

El Caracol at Chichén Itzá"

What are Venus's cycles? The planet Venus is known as the "morning star" and the "evening star," and the ancient Maya knew it was the same celestial body. Venus and our planet move through their orbits in a way that Venus appears on the horizon just before the sun rises at certain times of the year. The timing changes yearly, as Venus is the second planet from the sun while Earth is the third, so our planet takes longer to complete an orbit.

Each day after first appearing on the horizon at dawn, Venus rises a bit earlier. Then, it rises later until finally, one cannot see it at all. The process takes 263 days. Then, after fifty days of not being visible, Venus becomes the "evening star" for another 263 days. It fades again and can't be seen for eight days. The entire process takes 584 days, something the Maya knew precisely. They even had a myth to explain the cycle. Let's check it out!

The Myth of Chak Ek and the Star Wars

Chak Ek was the morning and evening star (the planet Venus) that spent the night in the underworld but arose shortly before dawn on the eastern sea's horizon. Shortly after Chak Ek rose into the sky, K'inich Ahau, the sun, arose. His brilliance dimmed Chak Ek until he could no longer be seen, filling the planet with jealousy. Chak Ek angrily plotted his revenge. He attacked K'inich Ahau's allies with his spear-thrower.

First, he attacked **K'awiil**, the god of food, fertility, lightning, and snakes. When he struck K'awiil with his dart, the people had no food, and chaos ensued. Fortunately, K'awiil reincarnated, and the people had food and peace once again. However, 584 days later, after the morning star passed through a complete cycle, Chak Ek was up to mischief again.

Every night, K'inich Ahau turned into a jaguar and passed through the underworld. Chak Ek speared the jaguar at the end of the dry season just as he arose on the eastern horizon. With a wounded sun, the world plunged into war. Next, Chak Ek cut off the head of One Hunahpu, the maize god, during the harvest season. He sent him to the underworld, leaving the people with no corn. However, three months later, One Hunahpu exploded out of the underworld through the Seven Water Cave, the place of new beginnings. He brought food to the people once again.

Ak ná ak (Ac ek), the Turtle Stars (the constellation Gemini or Orion), rose in the sky at the summer solstice, but Chak Ek knocked him out of the sky, burying the sun, corn, and people under the Earth. However, one of the Hero Twins arose and created new people. Yet, when a stranger from the west appeared in the dry season, Chak Ek killed him, bringing catastrophe to the world again. This cycle of chaos and order continued with the cycle of the planet Venus.

The Maya related a series of wars to this struggle during the cycles of Chak Ek in the heavens. They noticed that the great wars happened most often when Venus was rising in the evening (although this time changed yearly). Another factor was a solar eclipse in 743 CE. The Maya had a glyph, or a symbol, for these "star wars," representing the overturning of one ruling dynasty by another. The first known "star war" raged in 562 CE between the city-states of Tikal and Caracol. Tikal lost the war and became a ghost town for 120 years before it rose from the ashes.

King Yajaw Chan Muwaan of Bonampak and his captives[38]

In 631 CE, the city-states of Naranjo and Calakmul engaged in a fierce war, which Naranjo lost. The warriors of Calakmul tortured the enemy king to death. In 743 CE, the city-state of El Peru fell to Tikal one day after a solar eclipse. The vibrant murals of Bonampak illustrated a star war between Bonampak (a vassal of Calakmul) and the nearby city-state of Yaxchilan (allied with Tikal).

How Did the Maya Align Their Ceremonial Centers with the Sun?

The jungle has reclaimed many Maya cities, but using lidar imaging technology, researchers recently found hundreds of ancient cities that no one knew existed. The scholars were amazed that most aligned with the Maya 260-day festival calendar. By at least 1100 BCE, Maya cities on Mexico's Gulf Coast were oriented to where the sun rises or sets on particular dates. They also frequently had a grouping of twenty structures, probably alluding to the twenty months of Tzolk'in. The alignment of these cities shows the Maya were likely using their calendar for about 1,000 years before their earliest-known writing.

One ancient Maya city, Aguada Fénix in Tabasco, Mexico, near Guatemala's border, was built between 1100 and 800 BCE. Its ceremonial center was on an artificial plateau of clay and dirt almost a mile long and fifty feet high. It has a larger volume than the Great Pyramid of Giza, Egypt. Aguada Fénix was oriented north-south so that it lined up with the sunrise on May 9 or 10. What is unique about this day? In this part of Mesoamerica, it is "zenith day," when the sun is directly overhead, or at its zenith in the sky.

However, the researchers found different orientations in other cities. The most widespread orientation among lowland Maya cities built in the same period as Aguada Fénix was an alignment with the sunrises on February 11 and October 29. What's so special about those dates? Scholars aren't sure. However, the number of days between them is 260, the precise number of days in the Maya Tzolk'in festival calendar.

Roundup Activity: True or False?

Mark each statement with a T or F. Check your answers in the back of the book.

1. ( ) The god Hunahpu introduced the calendar to humans.

2. ( ) The Tzolk'in was the Maya religious or festival calendar.

3. ( ) The Maya had lunar months of about 30 days.

4. ( ) The Calendar Round coordinated the solar and festival calendars.

5. ( ) The Maya date of creation was 3114 BCE.

6. ( ) 2012 CE was when a new "Long Count" began for the Maya.

7. ( ) El Caracol at Chichén Itzá was an observatory to track Venus's cycles.

8. ( ) The Maya "star wars" involved competition between Saturn and the sun.

9. ( ) Aguada Fénix lined up with the sunrise on zenith day.

10. ( ) Many early Maya cities aligned with the sunrise on two dates 260 days apart.

Chapter 5: Glyphs of Power: Reading the Ancient Scripts

This chapter dives into the enigmatic world of hieroglyphics, the writing system the Maya used to record their history, mythology, and rituals. How long ago did the Maya start writing? How did their writing system work? Who was the teenager who made a stunning breakthrough in reading the Maya glyphs? Let's explore the fascinating Maya writing that opens a window into their intriguing culture.

Who Were the First Writers in Mesoamerica?

The Olmecs were the first complex civilization and the first writers in North America. Their culture flourished in today's Tabasco and Veracruz near Mexico's Gulf Coast. They built North America's first city and first pyramid. They introduced rubber balls and chocolate to the world. The Olmecs were avid tradespeople who traveled along the river system five hundred miles southeast into Guatemala and four hundred miles northwest into the Basin of Mexico. That means they would have interacted with the Maya.

The Olmec writing was primitive hieroglyphics, which used stylized pictures (glyphs) of objects to represent words or sounds. Some hieroglyphs were simple drawings of nouns, like corn, dog, or monkey. Others may have represented sounds. The first known writing was on the foot-long Cascajal Block found near the first Olmec city of San Lorenzo. It dates to around 900 BCE and has sixty-two symbols, or glyphs, in horizontal rows. Some of the Olmec glyphs are easy to identify, such as corn, torch, insect, pineapple, and fish. Others are more unclear. However, they seem to suggest religion and sacrificial rituals.

What glyphs can you identify on the Cascajal Block?[39]

About two hundred miles south of the Olmec heartland, the Zapotec people emerged as a complex civilization by 1300 BCE. We can determine they were writing with simple glyphs by 650 BCE from a carving with two glyphs that was found on a monument in San José Mogote. The glyphs are between a sacrificial victim's legs and read "earthquake," which was the seventeenth day in the Zapotec twenty-day month. These glyphs strongly suggest that the Zapotecs were writing and using a calendar at that point. Around 500 BCE, the Zapotecs of the Monte Albán area developed Mesoamerica's first complex hieroglyphics. Their **logo-syllabic system** used symbols representing a word or syllables of a word.

Zapotec glyphs for "earthquake" between the victim's legs[10]

When Did the Maya First Start Writing?

The first evidence of Maya writing is at San Bartolo, in the mountains of Guatemala. San Bartolo has a pyramid in which archaeologists discovered a treasure trove of murals depicting mythological scenes from the *Popol Vuh* and other stories. Among the murals of the maize god are the glyphs for the date "Seven Year." The glyphs date to between 400 and 200 BCE and are the first written reference to the Maya calendar. Archaeologists found multiple glyphs in the pyramid. However, the only other glyph the scholars could translate was "ajaw" (lord). This proves the Maya had a well-established writing system at that point, but it was somewhat different from the one they used later.

As the centuries passed, the Maya hieroglyphics evolved into a mature system with up to five hundred glyphs for words and sounds. The Maya covered a vast swathe of Mesoamerica and had different languages, although in the same Mayan language family. Thus, their glyphs for certain words varied a bit from place to place. The Maya writing was everywhere—on stone monuments, altars, doorways, pillars, and pottery. They also had books written on accordion folds of deerskin or paper made from bark. These books had jaguar-skin covers and recorded their genealogies, religion, myths, and history. The accordion-folded books are called *codices* (singular: *codex*).

After the Spaniards arrived in the 1500s, they destroyed most of the Maya books, believing they were full of false gods and demons. Only a handful of these books survived the book burnings. The oldest was the *Dresden Codex*. The book that survived was probably written in the eleventh or twelfth century CE, based on books from hundreds of years earlier. The *Grolier Codex* was written in the thirteenth century CE, and the *Paris Codex* about a century later. The fourth book was the *Madrid Codex*, written in the fifteenth century, decades before the Spaniards arrived.

This page from the Dresden Codex has columns of Maya glyphs, followed by a row of numbers and three Maya deities.[31]

What Are the Basics of the Maya Script?

Some glyphs in the Maya logo-syllabic script were *logograms*, representing whole words. The logograms usually represented nouns (like "mountain" or "cloud") or action verbs (like "dance" or "write"). Other glyphs were *phonograms (syllabograms)* that represented adjectives, prepositions, and single-syllable sounds, like "ta" or "ki." The

Maya writing system had up to five hundred glyphs. However, some of the glyphs changed appearance over the centuries.

By the late 1900s, linguists had figured out the meaning of about 60 percent of Maya glyphs, but they knew how to pronounce 80 percent. How could they pronounce a glyph without knowing its meaning? If the linguists knew the sounds represented by phonograms, they could pronounce the word (or at least part of it) without knowing what it meant. Comparably, you might see an English word you don't know, but you can make a stab at pronouncing it based on the consonants and vowels in the word. (Of course, that gets complicated with English because it's a combination of several languages, so we have "to," "two," and "too" all pronounced the same.)

Most of the Maya glyphs had two or three parts. The largest part was the main sign. If it were a noun or action verb, the Maya used a pictograph for the main sign. They used glyph symbols if the primary word was an adjective or preposition. The smaller parts of a glyph were *affixes*, which changed the primary word. For instance, they might make a noun plural or change the tense of a verb (like we would add "ed" or "ing" to a verb or change "make" to "made").

Reading the Maya glyphs had an interesting twist. They were usually written in columns and rows. The reader would typically read the first two glyphs on the top row, starting from the left. Then, the reader dropped down to the next row and read the first two glyphs in that row. He or she would continue with that pattern until reaching the bottom of the columns. Then the reader would return to the top row, read glyphs three and four in that row, and continue down.

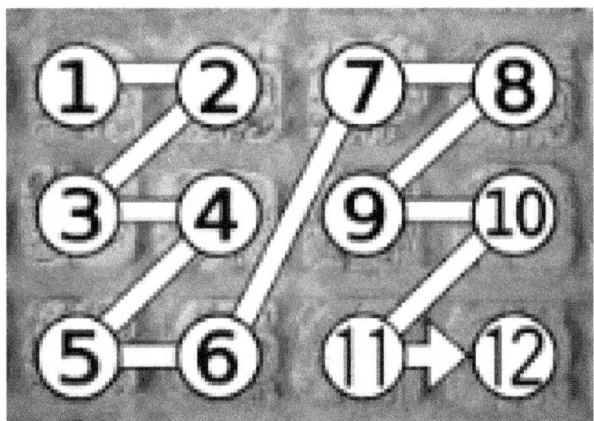

The Maya reading pattern[33]

Many of the Maya inscriptions on monuments announced something that happened on a specific date, so their word order was usually date/verb/subject. The most common pronoun describing a verb was the third person singular (he, his, she, her, it, its). The Maya attached pronouns directly to the verb glyph as affixes. To clarify gender, they used the prefix "aj" for males and "ix" for females as affixes on nouns.

What Were the Monumental Breakthroughs in Deciphering Maya Glyphs?

Before the Spanish conquest, the Maya priests instructed the boys and some girls from upper-class families to read and write. After conquering Maya lands, the Spaniards discouraged speaking in Mayan and tried to force everyone to speak Spanish. The Spaniards continued to educate the boys from elite families. However, they taught them to read and write Spanish with the alphabet we use today. Within a generation or two, most Maya no longer knew how to read their ancient language.

For centuries, the Maya glyphs on monuments, artwork, pottery, and codices were a mystery. No one knew what they meant. As we said, eventually linguists could decipher the meaning of about 60 percent of the glyphs. Recently, they had a breakthrough thanks to an exceptionally bright teenager, and now they can read 90 percent of the Maya writings. What led to these great leaps forward?

In the 1500s, when the Spaniards were conquering Mexico, Commander Hernán Cortés acquired a copy of the *Dresden Codex*, probably at Chichén Itzá. He shipped it to Charles V, Holy Roman Emperor of Austria and King of Spain. The codex was placed in the Royal Library of Dresden, where it was ignored for two centuries. Finally, parts of it were published. It was placed in a basement for safekeeping when bombing was going on in World War II. Unfortunately, the basement flooded, and it was severely damaged. Fortunately, scholars and artists had made earlier copies in the 1800s.

Using five pages of the *Dresden Codex*, a brilliant eccentric named Constantine Rafinesque cracked the code to Maya numerals in 1832.

In 1880, the *Dresden Codex* was still at the Royal Library of Dresden. The library also had the *de Landa Alphabet*, a partial translation of Maya glyphs by a Catholic priest in the Yucatán in the sixteenth century that had been rediscovered in the nineteenth century.

Using both texts, a librarian named Ernst Förstemann unlocked the Maya astronomy tables and the Calendar Round. After this breakthrough, scholars knew how to convert the Maya dates inscribed on monuments to our dating system.

Linguists continued trying to decipher the Maya glyphs. They got a bit derailed by wrongly assuming that each of the parts of a glyph represented a complete word. They thought one glyph could be a combination of two or three words. Now, linguists know that most glyphs represent only one word, and the other parts are the affixes that make a word plural, change the verb tense, and so on.

In 1952, a Russian linguist named Yuri Knorozov realized that the approximately five hundred Maya glyphs couldn't be an alphabet because there were too many of them. They couldn't all stand for single words because too few existed. He correctly decided the Maya glyphs were a combination of words and sounds. In 1973, thirty scholars met in Palenque, Mexico, to study the "Tablet of Ninety-six Glyphs." They were able to translate enough of the tablet to discover that it was a chronicle of the lives of six Maya kings of Palenque.

In 1981, fifteen-year-old David Stuart, the son of an archaeologist working in Mexico and Guatemala, figured out that individual glyphs could be written in a dozen ways. He contributed immeasurably to the content and structure of Maya hieroglyphics, deciphering many new syllables and logograms. His work helped linguists forge ahead in understanding Maya writing over the next three decades.

What Are Some Examples of Maya Inscriptions?

The jaguar played a vital role in Maya mythology. For instance, the sun transformed into a jaguar when it passed through the underworld at night. As mentioned, the Maya had different glyphs or variations of a glyph for the same word. The Mayan word for jaguar was *balam*. Sometimes, they wrote this by drawing a jaguar head facing left with a fang protruding from his jaw. Other times, they added a phonetic affix on the left to give the sound clue for "ba." The "ba" figure was a rounded square with a large hole at the top.

Glyph for jaguar (balam) with "ba" sound and a jaguar head[83]

The glyph for the grumpy goddess Ixchel has two parts. The main glyph on the right side is a caricature of the scowling deity, with her usual grimace and trademark long, hooked nose. The smaller affix on the left is the glyph for "red"–*chak*. No one today is quite sure why that is part of her glyph. It might be acting as a phonetic clue for *chel*. Or, she may have been called "Chak Chel" in some Maya areas.

Glyph for the goddess Ixchel[84]

Roundup Activity: Multiple Choice

Check your answers in the back of the book.

1. The first writers in North America were:
   a. The Aztecs
   b. The Maya
   c. The Olmecs
   d. The Zapotecs

2. How many glyphs are on the Cascajal Block?
   a. 20
   b. 31
   c. 62
   d. 90

3. What did the Zapotec glyphs between a sacrificial victim's legs read?
   a. Earthquake
   b. Hurricane
   c. Tornado
   d. Tsunami

4. Where were the first known Maya glyphs found?
   a. Calakmul
   b. Chichén Itzá
   c. San Bartolo
   d. Tikal

5. What part of the Maya logo-syllabic script represented whole words, like water or mountain?
   a. Logograms
   b. Phonograms
   c. Syllabograms
   d. All the above

6. What were the smaller parts of a glyph that changed the word, such as making it plural or in the past tense?
   a. Affixes
   b. Prefixes
   c. Suffixes
   d. None of the above

7. How did the Maya usually read their hieroglyphics?
   a. Horizontally or across the page from left to right, like we do
   b. Vertically or moving down a column
   c. Horizontally for two glyphs and then down to the next row
   d. Horizontally, but from right to left

8. Who cracked the code to Maya numerals in 1832?
   a. Charles V
   b. Cortés
   c. Knorozov
   d. Rafinesque

9. What teenager made stunning breakthroughs in reading Maya glyphs in the 1980s?
   a. Charles V
   b. David Stuart
   c. Hernán Cortés
   d. Yuri Knorozov

Chapter 6: Tikal, the City of Gods

Tucked among northern Guatemala's rolling hills and rainforests, Tikal's breathtaking temples soared above the greenery. What made Tikal so remarkable? It was home to at least 50,000 people, maybe twice that many. It was one of the oldest Maya cities, springing up around 600 BCE and flourishing for 1,500 years. Tikal ruled over smaller cities and towns, spreading hundreds of miles. It had a sophisticated water system with dams, reservoirs, and sand filtration to clean the drinking water.

How were the ruins of Tikal discovered? When the Spaniards arrived in the 1500s, Tikal had been a ghost town for six hundred years. The Spanish conquistadors never found it. Jungle vines and towering trees covered most of the massive pyramids. Yet, rumors of a mysterious and magical city hidden in the jungle swirled. Finally, in 1848, the local Maya people led government officials to the ancient ruins. Archaeologists have been exploring and restoring the stunning city ever since. Today, thousands of tourists clamber over the breathtaking ruins each year.

Why was Tikal's location sacred? What was its cosmic symbolism? How did a distant city influence Tikal's temples and mythology? Let's explore!

What Was the Cosmic Symbolism of Tikal Layout and Architecture?

The towering Tikal pyramids may have symbolized the connection between the earthly realm and the heavens. The ancient Maya didn't call their city "Tikal." That was a name given it by the nineteenth-century Maya, meaning "at the reservoir." The low areas of Tikal are boggy and might have once been a lake. In ancient times, the Maya called it "Mutal." That might mean "tied up," as the glyph for "mut" shows a man's hair tied back in a man-bun. "Mutal" might also mean "whispering" or "voices" in the Petén-Mayan language. One can imagine hearing the whispers of the Maya gods while wandering through the pyramids.

Tikal landscape[85]

The remnants of 3,000 buildings still stand in Tikal. The temple complexes are in nine groupings of plazas and pyramids built on the hills rising above the swampland. The ancient Maya constructed causeways and bridges connecting the sacred areas, which spread over 500 acres. The many pyramids in Tikal were related to the Maya religious calendar.

In the late 600s CE, the Maya began building a new twin pyramid complex each k'atun, the sacred twenty-year period. They kept building them until shortly before the city died. Archaeologists have uncovered nine twin-pyramid complexes so far. These pyramids had flat tops with staircases rising on each side. A plaza in the middle of the twin pyramids was aligned north and south.

King Jasaw Kaan K'awil (Sky Rain) built the first of these twin pyramid complexes to celebrate a stunning victory over the rival city-state of Calakmul. Sky Rain had become the *ajaw,* or king, in 682 CE. Before his reign, King Sky Witness of Calakmul (the "Snake Kingdom") defeated Tikal in 572 CE. This was one of the infamous "star wars" between the superpowers. Tikal barely survived but limped along for the next century. King B'alaj Chan K'awiil of Dos Pilas, an ally of Calakmul, attacked Tikal in 679 CE. He captured and sacrificed Tikal's king, Shield Skull, who was his own brother.

When Sky Rain finally defeated Calakmul in 695 CE, Tikal surged ahead in power and influence. Sky Rain ruled for fifty-two years and built two twin pyramid complexes during his long reign to celebrate his star wars victories.

Sky Rain also built the Temple of the Great Jaguar (Temple One) around 730 CE. With steep sides, it is the height of a fourteen-story building. Why is it called the Jaguar Temple? A carving on a wooden beam at the pyramid's peak shows the king sitting on a jaguar throne, which represented divine kingship. The Maya considered their kings the earthly representatives of K'inich Ahau, the sun god, who turned into a jaguar at night.

Tikal's Temple of the Jaguar[36]

The Maya buried Sky Rain in a tomb under the Temple of the Great Jaguar, wearing jade earplugs, bracelets, and anklets. A pearl and jade necklace hung around his neck, and he lay on jaguar pelts. Also in the tomb were some bones with carvings into which the artisans had rubbed cinnabar, a red mercury sulfide.

The Cosmic Canoe

Sky Rain's tomb held two human bones with carvings representing a fundamental Maya myth: "Crossing the Milky Way in the Cosmic Canoe." The scene on one of the bones shows a canoe with its passengers: Iguana, Monkey, Parrot, and Peccary. They represent the constellations and mourn the dead maize god (One Hunahpu). The gods Stingray (Day) and Old Jaguar (Night) paddle the cosmic canoe carrying the dead god across the Milky Way to the center of the cosmos. The Milky Way is the serpent or dragon whose mouth is the center of the universe.

The scene on the second bone shows the passengers screaming as their canoe upends. The Milky Way has turned, appearing to tip toward the earth. The maize god is flung out of the canoe and lands on the turtle constellation (Orion). The maize god flings kernels of corn into the sky. They become the Pleiades but drift to earth in the spring to grow corn, representing the maize god's rebirth.

What Made Tikal's Location Sacred?

Tikal's location in the Maya lowlands was not arbitrary. The Maya chose it for its spiritual and symbolic significance. The towering Yax Che ("First Tree") ceiba, or kapok, trees dominated the rainforests around Tikal. They held deep spiritual significance for the Maya, who thought the trees symbolized the universe. The Yax Che was the "World Tree," with roots descending to Xibalba and branches reaching the thirteen levels of heaven. The Maya believed this sacred tree was the portal between heaven, Earth, and the underworld. It transported the souls of the dead to the afterlife.

Sacred Yax Che (ceiba) tree from Codex Fejéváry-Mayer[87]

As previously mentioned, the Maya often aligned their cities with the sunrise on special days. Other times, they lined them up with other astronomical or geographical features of spiritual importance. How did that play out for Tikal? The oldest pyramid is the "Lost World" (Mundo Perdido) temple. The Maya built it around 600 BCE over the rubbish of an earlier structure. It connects to the East Pyramid, and these two structures are Tikal's oldest buildings. The Lost World temple is one hundred feet high and built with masonry blocks almost six feet long. It was one of the first Maya compounds with astronomical alignment.

The Lost World temple area was an *"E-Group" astronomical complex*. E-Groups were ceremonial buildings the Maya built as observatories. Remember, they believed the planets, stars, and sun were gods. The Lost World complex marked sunrises on March 11 and October 2. Its east stairway was the observation point for sunrises. The first three pyramids on the east platform of the complex marked the sun's progress at the equinox and solstice. The nearby palace of Jaguar Paw the Great faces west, marking sunsets on March 31 and September 12. It's possible that the two "observatories" worked together in a calendar for spring planning and fall harvest.

What Was the Link Between Teotihuacan and Tikal?

The two great cities of Teotihuacan and Tikal were eight hundred miles apart, yet they had a strong association. The gigantic city of Teotihuacan ruled central Mexico from 200 BCE to 600 CE.

Who were some of the gods that both cities worshiped? They included the rain god, the feathered serpent, the "old man" god, a jaguar god, and the sun and moon. The two cities exchanged ideas about mythology, religious rituals, and temple architecture.

What brought these two cities together? They were trade partners. Teotihuacan was eager for goods from the rainforest. They loved cacao beans for making chocolate, quetzal bird feathers, and jaguar pelts. The Maya had their own neighborhood in the middle of Teotihuacan, and Tikal had a Teotihuacan temple complex. Yet, the friendly relationship went sour. Teotihuacan invaded Tikal and ruled the city for about a century.

David Stuart translated the inscriptions on a monument in Tikal. They told the story of a Teotihuacan general named Siyaj K ak (Fire is Born), who conquered Tikal in 378 CE. Tikal's king, Jaguar Paw, died the same day, most likely killed by the Teotihuacanos. Spearthrower Owl was the king of Teotihuacan at that time. General Fire is Born crowned First Crocodile (Yax Nuun Ayiin) as Tikal's new king. He was the son of Spearthrower Owl.

What else was on the monument? It spoke of the "paddlers" from the cosmic canoe myth, who carried the maize god into the universe. Stuart said it also mentioned a date, which was half of a k'atun, the sacred twenty-year unit. The inscriptions said the gods were "half-diminished" at that time. Apparently, in the Maya idea of time, the gods grew smaller and weaker as the twenty years passed. Then, they renewed and regenerated at the beginning of a new k'atun.

The inscriptions also said that Storm Sky, son of First Crocodile, was the next king of Tikal. They described him as the metaphorical caretaker of time and of the gods. His job was to look after them, especially in their time of weakness. He had to assist them through this dangerous period and help them regain their strength when the new k'atun began.

First Crocodile died in 404 BCE. He was buried in Tikal's Lost World complex, and nine people were sacrificed to attend to him in Xibalba. A cup with the inscription "Spearthrower Owl's son" lay beside the body. Also in the tomb was a ceramic incense burner in the shape of a god, possibly Chaac or the Teotihuacan "Old God," sitting on a stool made from human bones.

Incense burner from First Crocodile's tomb[88]

Intriguingly, an isotype analysis of First Crocodile's remains indicates that he did not grow up in Teotihuacan. (Isotype analysis gives information about what a person ate in their lifetime.) The man buried in the tomb grew up in northern Guatemala, in or around Tikal. Was he an imposter pretending to be a prince? Or did the Teotihuacan king's son grow up in Tikal for some reason?

First Crocodile may or may not have been a Teotihuacan prince. Nevertheless, the Mexican city left its mark on Tikal long before his birth.

In 2016, lidar technology showed something unexpected. What everyone thought was a group of hills was actually an unknown temple structure. As they uncovered it, scholars got excited. It was a miniature copy of Teotihuacan's Feathered Serpent Pyramid. The Maya began building it around 300 CE—almost eight decades before the Teotihuacan takeover.

The Temple of the Feathered Serpent was Teotihuacan's most striking pyramid. Heads of the feathered serpent and the googly-eyed rain god jutted out from its sides. The Tikal version was about 30 percent smaller and decorated with green obsidian glass from Teotihuacan. The Tikal temple was oriented fifteen degrees east of true north, similar to Teotihuacan's Feathered Serpent.

At the North Acropolis in the center of Tikal is Temple 33, also in Teotihuacan style. It was a burial pyramid for Storm Sky, son of First Crocodile. It featured enormous masonry and stucco masks, larger than a man.

Stucco mask, perhaps of the rain god or Itzamná, on Temple 33[89]

How Was Tikal a Religious and Ritual Center?

Tikal was a regional center of religious and ritual activities. Tikal's North Acropolis had over one hundred stone temples, constantly enlarged and rebuilt. The Maya conducted ceremonies and sacrifices at its temple pyramids and plazas.

Enormous masks of mythological deities flanked the pyramids' stairs. The wide steps served as a stage for ritual performances by the Maya priests and kings. The rituals were deeply intertwined with Maya mythology, and their purpose was to maintain harmony between the natural and supernatural worlds. These rituals included burning incense, bloodletting using stingray spines, and human sacrifice. The Maya also offered food and drink to the gods.

Maya prayers and rituals revolved around their belief that they were sinful. They thought the forces of the universe determined their fate. They humbly approached the gods, knowing their deities could give them good or bad fortune. The gods could punish people for their sins by sending hunger and sickness. Alternatively, they could provide people with good health, harvests, and hunting. If the Maya wanted to build a house or go on a hunting expedition, they would consult their priests about when to start. The priests used their knowledge of astrology and foreseeing the future to tell them the best days.

Rituals at Tikal also involved burials. Among many notable tombs, Burial 160 in Tikal's North Acropolis became famous for a jade mask found there. A man, probably a ruler, lay in the tomb with the mosaic jade mask on his chest. Horrifyingly, two teen boys were sacrificed in the tomb before it was sealed, probably to serve the lord in the afterlife.

Replica of a jade mosaic mask from Burial 160 at Tikal[40]

Decline

Around 950 CE, Tikal's people abruptly abandoned their enchanting city. It became the lost city for nine centuries. The same thing happened to most of the Maya cities in Guatemala. Several northern Maya cities, like Chichén Itzá in the Yucatán Peninsula, continued to flourish until the Spaniards arrived in the 1500s. What happened to Tikal and the rest of the southern Maya? Some theories include the unending warfare between rival cities, overpopulation, deforestation, and natural disasters like drought, earthquakes, or hurricanes.

Roundup Activity: Comprehension Questions

1. How did the layout and architecture of Tikal reflect Maya cosmology and religious beliefs?

_____
_____
_____
_____

2. Why was Tikal's location considered spiritually significant to the ancient Maya?

_____
_____
_____
_____

3. How did the Teotihuacanos influence Maya temples?

_____
_____
_____
_____

4. What Maya myth was inscribed on human bones in Sky Rain's tomb?

_____
_____
_____
_____

5. Around what beliefs did Maya prayers and rituals revolve?

_____
_____
_____
_____

Chapter 7: Beliefs, Rituals, and the Cycle of Life and Death

The Maya rituals and ceremonies celebrated the cycle of life and death, demonstrating their profound connection to the divine. How did they celebrate the birth of a baby and coming of age? What about weddings and funerals? What did they think happened in the afterlife? Why did they worship their ancestors? Let's find out!

What is a Dualistic Concept of the Universe?

Cosmology is one's understanding of the universe and how everything connects. It involves beliefs about how the universe came into being and how it became what it is now. The Maya cosmology was *dualistic*, meaning they saw things as pairs, or parallel, even if seemingly opposite or contrasting. These opposite ideas, like male and female, dark and light, and life and death, were all necessary parts of the whole.

Many of the Maya deities were twins, like the Monkey Twins, the Hero Twins, and their father and uncle, One Hunahpu and Seven Hunahpu. Other gods had opposite or conflicting characteristics. For instance, Chaac graciously brought rain, but he also demanded child sacrifice and brought hail and hurricanes. K'inich Ahau, the sun god, brought warmth and light, but he was also a war god.

How Did They Celebrate a Baby's Birth?

The ancient Maya rejoiced over a baby's birth. They believed babies brought wealth and good luck. In the naming ceremony, a shaman sprinkled rainwater on the infant while burning incense. He gave the newborn a name based on the day they were born in the Tzolk'in (religious) calendar. Babies also had nicknames unrelated to the calendar. After naming the child, the shaman foretold his or her future.

Many upper-class Maya showed their status and kinship through the custom of *cranial modification*, in which they changed the shape of an infant's skull. They placed padded wooden frames on their babies' heads so their foreheads sloped and they became cone headed. The babies wore these frames until they were toddlers or older. The Maya explained to Spanish priests that their gods told them to do this so they would be noble. They also believed it prevented babies from losing their souls.

Types of headframes[41]

The Maya in the Yucatán Peninsula had a ceremony called *Hetzmek*, or "breaking the baby's legs." Don't worry! It wasn't as brutal as it sounds. When a baby was a newborn, the adults bundled the child and carried him or her in their arms. At three or four months old, the mother started carrying the baby on her hip. This called for a ceremony where one of the elders would open the baby's legs. Everyone gathered at the family's home for the festivities.

Until then, the baby would only drink breastmilk, but at the ceremony, the baby tasted its first cornmeal paste and boiled egg. The Maya believed that opening the legs helped "open the mind" to develop into a hardworking and moral person. They also thought that straddling the mother's hip enabled the child to walk a long way without pain when they were older. Some Maya still practice this ceremony today.

How Was "Coming of Age" Celebrated?

Maya boys and girls had several rituals as they passed from childhood into their teens. Around age twelve, the girls celebrated puberty by reciting the rules of correct behavior and confessing their shortcomings. They had a ritual water cleansing, then removed the string of red shells they had worn around their waists since they were toddlers. In its place, a teen girl wore a string with one white shell around her waist to indicate she was becoming a woman. Maya teen girls continued living with their parents until they married at age fifteen to seventeen.

The boy's coming-of-age ceremony took place when he was fourteen or fifteen. First, he had to go hunting and bring home an animal he had killed to show he was ready to be a Maya man. Then, he went through a bloodletting ritual. He had to pierce his tongue, lip, or private parts with a stingray spine and let the blood drip onto a piece of bark paper or into a little bowl. Once he proved himself a man, his parents threw a big party. At this point, he painted his face black and moved into a dormitory for unmarried teen males. He lived there until he got married around age eighteen or nineteen.

What Was a Maya Wedding Like?

Marriages were not love matches. If a young man and woman independently decided they wanted to marry each other, everyone else thought it was weird. The custom was for a matchmaker to arrange a marriage. Teens were supposed to marry someone from their own village or town and in the same social class. Once both sets of parents agreed to a match, the groom's parents would provide clothing for the bride as a bride price.

The marriage ceremony was simple and usually took place in the home of the bride's parents. The priest or shaman gave a speech that explained the marriage covenant. Then, he lit incense and pronounced prayers and a blessing over the couple. After that, the two families and other guests sat down to a feast prepared by the bride's family. The groom moved in with his new wife's parents and worked for them for the next six or seven years. The young wife had to serve food and drink to her new husband to show she recognized the marriage.

Dances That Portrayed Mythology

Dance is an integral part of almost every culture, yet for the Maya, it was more than a fun pastime. For them, dances told stories. The "Humul" dancers used special movements and wore lightweight racks on their backs with bamboo and feathers forming symbols. Some dancers portrayed supernatural spirits and their interactions with the natural world. Others portrayed animals. Some of the dances ended with human sacrifice.

Bonampak mural of Humul dancers with feather racks on their backs[48]

How Did the Maya View Life and Death as a Cycle?

The Maya thought life and death were cyclical, similar to how they viewed time. The many Maya subgroups did not all share the same mythology or concept of the afterlife. They all believed in life after death yet differed on what that life was like. The *Popol Vuh* said that some of the gods who died, like the maize god and Hunahpu, either reincarnated in a different form or came back to life in the same form. Other gods, like Seven Macaw, seemed to stay dead. The Maya did not think of death as the end. Some Maya believed in reincarnation for certain people. However, they almost all believed everyone went to Xibalba for at least a while.

Why Did the Maya Practice Human Sacrifice?

In the ancient Maya belief system, sacrifice bought the gods' favor. They sacrificed many things, like flowers, corn, rubber, jade, birds, and dogs. They also offered human sacrifices. Often, this was a type of execution for someone who had committed a crime worthy of death. Other times, the Maya sacrificed enemy warriors they had captured. However, they also sacrificed children and innocent people.

Human sacrifice ramped up dramatically in the Post-Classic period, which began around 900 CE. This was when much of the southern Maya world collapsed. Toltec colonists moving into the Yucatán Peninsula from central Mexico might have influenced the increased human sacrifice. Some of the Maya even continued human sacrifice after the Spanish conquest, when they mixed Catholicism with their traditional belief system.

What Was Xibalba Like?

Xibalba literally means "scary place." The *Popol Vuh* gives us an idea of what the Maya underworld was like. The gods of death were capricious, deceptive, and cruel tyrants. The Maya believed caves were a way to get in and out of Xibalba, which was under the Earth's surface. It must not have been very far underground, or perhaps the gods of Xibalba had phenomenal hearing. How else could they hear folks playing ball in the world of the living? It seems the ball court of One Hunahpu and his clan was a portal to Xibalba, which might explain why the Lords of Death could hear them playing.

Twelve lords ruled Xibalba, working in pairs. One Death and Seven Death were the top rulers. The other ten were demons who caused suffering, sickness, and death among people in the land of the living. Xibalba was full of lesser gods, monsters, and creatures like the messenger owls, who followed the demands of the twelve lords.

Ah Puch (One Death), one of the head Lords of Death[48]

The *Popol Vuh* mentions various places in Xibalba, like the rivers and canyons at the entrance, the council hall where the Lords of Death gathered, and the houses of horror, such as Bat House and Jaguar House. Xibalba also had outdoor areas, like a ball court and gardens, which seems improbable in a place without the sun's light.

Xibalba was a place of testing, with many perils. If a person (or god) failed a test, they might be doomed to remain in Xibalba forever. It had nine levels through which a dead person had to navigate. People buried their loved ones with weapons, food, and chocolate to help them make their way through Xibalba. Dogs were the ultimate guide through the underworld, so they often buried ceramic or real dogs to help their masters.

What About Heaven?

The Maya believed in thirteen heavens resting on the back of a reptilian sea monster floating in the sea. The heavens were in layers and ruled by the god Oxlahun-ti-ku, who was thirteen gods in one. The Aztecs and other Mesoamerican cultures shared the idea of thirteen heavens in layers. The Maya believed the heavens were mainly a place for the gods to live.

Almost all humans and even gods went to Xibalba when they died. However, the Maya believed their earliest ancestors were gods who lived on a lower level of heaven and watched over them. The only people who went to heaven were those who died violent deaths. Examples are women who died in childbirth, men who died in battle or in a ball game, sacrificial victims, and people who committed suicide (which was considered a type of self-sacrifice).

What Happened When Someone Died?

When someone died, their family buried them with some corn in their mouth. They needed something to eat in Xibalba. The maize also represented rebirth and new life. The goal was to follow the maize god to reincarnation. Other times, they might put a jade bead in their mouth. Jade was used for money, and they would need to pay for things on their journey through the afterlife. Most Maya buried their family members under the floors of their homes.

When a king or other royalty died, the Maya adorned him or her with bracelets, necklaces, and a headdress. Then, they wrapped the body in a bundle and covered it with cinnabar (mercury-sulfate powder) before laying it in a tomb, usually under a pyramid. The Maya believed cinnabar reanimated the dead, as its red color was like blood and the heat of fire. In one tomb, archaeologists found a large pottery vessel holding the body of a noblewoman, apparently an alternative burial method.

The Maya placed stingray spines or other bloodletting tools in the tomb to enable the dead person to continue worshiping the gods. The Maya often sacrificed people and unceremoniously dumped them in the grave with a royal person. They were undoubtedly servants destined to continue looking after their master or mistress in the afterlife. They also sometimes laid a dead baby on the body of the royal person. Whether the child died naturally or was related to the dead person remains a mystery.

A funerary mask from Calakmul⁴⁴

A funerary mask, possibly meant to protect and guide the dead person, was often placed on the face or chest of a king. The Maya also sometimes placed animals like a crocodile or turtle in royal tombs. After closing the tomb, the Maya burned incense on it. The rising smoke symbolized the dead person's soul rising to join the ancestors. The body remained to give power to the temple in which it was buried.

What Was Ancestor Worship All About?

Sometimes, the Maya cremated a king or priest instead of burying him in a tomb. They put the ashes in an urn, sometimes buried in a tomb. However, they didn't always bury the urn. They sometimes kept it in a sacred place and put food in front of it on festival days to honor the dead person. Honoring the dead wasn't restricted to kings. Because they buried their dead under their houses, ordinary Maya considered their homes and land sacred. Consequently, they rarely sold their ancestral land. They believed that their ancestors guarded the boundaries.

Both royalty and commoners built cedarwood idols of their ancestors. They put some of the deceased's ashes in the figure and painted it blue. They considered them precious family heirlooms that they passed down through the family. The Maya worshiped male and female ancestors who had leadership positions when living. Sometimes, a Maya king would proclaim his ancestors to be gods and worship them as such. Of course, since he was their descendant, that meant he was also a deity. It was a way of exercising political control.

Roundup Activity: Fill in the Blank

Fill in the blanks with the words and phrases below. Check your answers in the back of the book.

| bloodletting | cinnabar | dualistic | Hetzmek |
| house | Humul | matchmaker | violent | Xibalba |

The Maya cosmology was _____, meaning they saw things as pairs or parallel. The _____ ceremony marked "breaking the baby's legs," when instead of being swaddled, he or she was carried straddling the mother's hip. A Maya teen boy had to go through a _____ ritual as part of his coming-of-age ceremony. A _____ arranged the marriage of a young Maya couple. _____ dancers wore big racks with feathers on their backs and portrayed Maya myths. The Maya believed almost everyone went to _____ when they died, although they might later be reincarnated. The only way to get into Maya heaven was to die a _____ death. Most Maya buried their family members under their _____. The Maya sprinkled _____ on their dead nobles, believing it reanimated the dead.

Chapter 8: Shamans and Their Magic

This chapter explores the mystical world of Maya shamans. How did they serve as intermediaries between humans and the realm of the gods? What did a person have to do to become a shaman? What were some typical rituals they performed? How did they connect with the spirit world?

What Did Shamans Do?

Shamans entered into trances, or altered states of consciousness, to communicate with their ancestors or the gods. They asked them for power to heal and insight to guide the kings or others who came to them for advice. Most Maya shamans specialized in certain areas. For instance, some shamans treated pain or illness through their extensive knowledge of medicinal herbs. Others cast the pain, sickness, or disability out of a person by exorcising the demon causing it. But not all shamans had this power. Some shamans used both herbal medicine and exorcism.

Before healing a patient, a shaman needed to diagnose the problem. Typically, he or she would begin chanting and enter into a trance to discern the illness or problem and what to do about it. Some shamans were so powerful in this area that they could spiritually discerned the diagnosis and treatment before the patient opened his mouth to explain what was happening.

Aside from healing, some shamans specialized in things like performing agriculture ceremonies during planting season to ensure a great harvest. They performed rituals to encourage Chaac to send rain. Shamans had many other roles, like advisers to the rulers. Like today's priests and pastors, they performed rituals and prayers for newborns, coming-of-age, weddings, and funerals.

Ceramic image of a Maya shaman[45]

Another specialty of shamans was putting a curse on someone. People who had been offended or harmed by someone would ask the shaman to help them get revenge. The shaman might look up an incantation in *Chilam Balam* (*The Book of the Jaguar Priest*). Sometimes, the shaman would place a circle of flowers near the person's home, where they were sure to walk. Then, the shaman would put a curse on that person, calling down a catastrophe.

Other shamans did the opposite. Instead of cursing people, they tried to stop curses that affected large populations. They would perform rituals and incantations to keep hurricanes, floods, earthquakes, and droughts away.

How Did the Shamans Train in Magic and Healing?

The Maya genuinely believed that their shamans had mystical powers and were their connection to the gods. The shamans had healing powers using Maya traditional medicine, purification rituals, and interceding with the spirit world. Of course, these skills and powers required rigorous training. How did a man or woman become a shaman? Did they simply decide that was something they wanted to do? Did other people or circumstances decide for them?

The Maya believed that some people were born to be shamans. Many Maya women could recognize specific signs when their child was still a fetus. They discerned certain ways of moving about and kicking in the womb, marking that child as a future shaman. To test it out, a mother would bury a piece of crystal or marble in the yard behind her cooking area. When the baby started walking, they would toddle straight to where the crystal was buried if they were destined to be a shaman. They would squat down and try to pry the crystal or marble out of the dirt with their little fingers. Children who were born with the gift of shamanism did not require future training.

A person who was not born with the gift trained to become a shaman by becoming an apprentice and helper to a shaman. It took years to acquire the knowledge and skills needed. There weren't formal classes. Instead, the shaman would have the apprentice watch him make herbal medicines or perform ceremonies. Throughout the day, the shaman spoke with his apprentice, explaining why he was doing what he was doing. After observing and listening, the apprentice gradually took on more responsibilities.

How Did They Practice Divination and Communicate with the Spirit World?

Shamans put themselves into a trance to communicate with the spirit world and have insight into the future. They did this in several ways. Some could go into a trance simply by praying, chanting, and burning incense. Other shamans performed dances, played drums, drank special teas, ate certain things, or smoked substances, most of which were hallucinogenic. They smoked *Nicotiana rustica*, a wild tobacco. It had a much higher nicotine content than today's tobacco and produced a mild high. The Maya shamans consumed peyote, a small, spineless cactus with hallucinogenic button-shaped growths, to have visions or hear spiritual voices. They believed it gave them insight. The shamans also believed spirits lived in morning glory plants because their seeds caused visions.

The cane toad (*Bufo marinus*) of Mesoamerica and South America grows at least six inches long and has poison glands that can kill dogs or other animals that eat it. It has a large gland behind each eye and other glands on its back that emit a bufotoxin if threatened. The toxin can kill humans or cause seizures if they eat the toad or take folk medicine with the toxin in it. However, the Maya shamans would put some of the bufotoxin into a cigar and smoke it, preferably in a cave, so that they could communicate with the dead in Xibalba. Of course, it was hazardous. Aside from potentially killing the shaman, the bufotoxin could cause lifelong mental health disorders and muscle coordination issues.

A Maya shaman smoking a cigar[46]

At ritual ceremonies, shamans ate k'aizalaj okox, hallucinogenic mushrooms that caused euphoria and detachment from the real world. They ate them fresh or dried them and made a powder. The mushrooms seemed linked with human sacrifice and Pok Ta' Pok, the Maya ball game. The shamans had visions but also heart palpitations when they ate these "magic mushrooms."

What Were Their Tools and Symbols?

Shamans used several objects to assist them in their work. One was a clear stone about two inches in diameter. Shamans often carried several in a pouch. They were useful for diagnosing illness, seeing into the future, and discerning a person's intentions. Another tool was a *balam* (jaguar), a term used for something sacred. These were clay figurines that the shamans arranged on an altar and called on when chanting. They were passed down among the Maya for hundreds of years.

A third tool was a sharpened human shin bone or a stingray spine. Shamans used these when placing a curse on someone. They would call that person to mind and use the bone or spine to "poke" the victim in a vulnerable spot. They never touched the person; it was all mental gymnastics, except the bone or spine was real. Another tool was the cross. No, not the Christian cross—the cross the Maya had before the Spaniards showed up. This one had four equal sides and represented the ceiba tree, or the "Tree of Life," that reached from Xibalba to the heavens. The top of the cross is heaven, the foot is earth, and the arms are wind and water. The shaman would sit with it when meditating for deeper awareness. Since the ceiba (kapok) was the most sacred tree, the shamans often performed rituals in its shade.

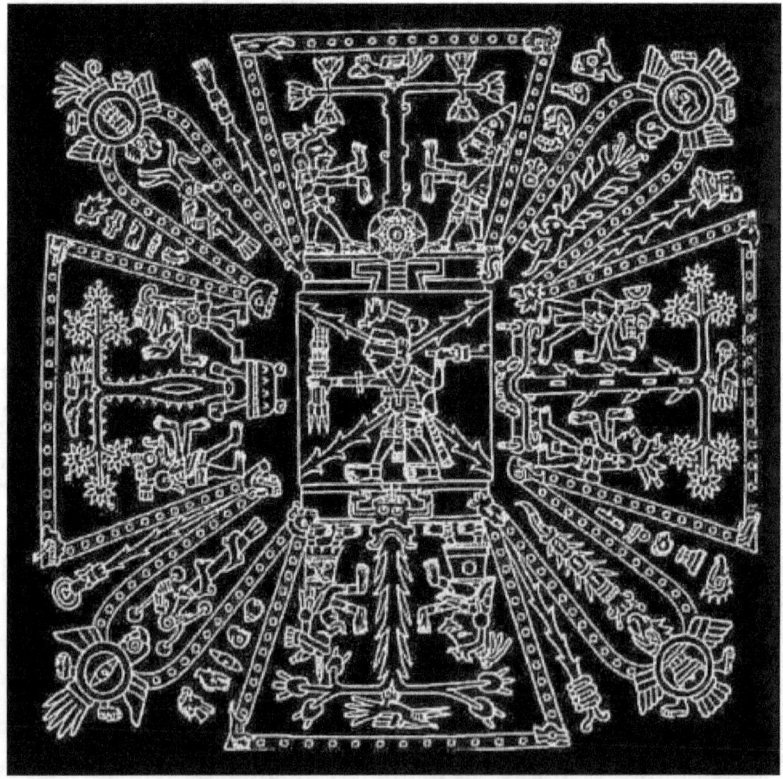

The Maya cross represents the ceiba tree.⁷

A *homa* was a small gourd the Maya used to drink *balché*, an alcoholic drink made from lilac tree bark and honey. Both the gourd and the drink were sacred tools of the shaman. A shaman would hang the homa gourds on each side of the door going into a sick person's room to cure the person and keep out the evil winds making the person ill. Everyone present drank the *balché*, which made them slightly intoxicated. However, the shaman often squirted it up his rectum, which made him empty his bowels and gave him hallucinations and visions.

Shamans used a special water called *Zuhuy Ha* in the Yucatan Mayan language. This "virgin water" came from a cenote or sinkhole. A Maya town called X-Colelbil Ek Tun (Lady Black Rock) was considered especially sacred as it had several cenotes where the water was close to the surface. Shamans traveled from miles away to collect the holy water from Lady Black Rock and would speak of the place in their chants.

Shamans used incense in most of their ceremonies, and their favorite was *pom*, made from the sap of the tall copal tree of the rainforest. The dried sap formed crystals, which went into an incense burner with charcoal.

The Maya shamans had several uses for the *zip che* shrub (*Bunchosia glandulosa*), called "peanut butter bush" today because its fruit smells and tastes like peanut butter. Shamans brewed tea from the fruit to make their patients strong and boost their sex drive. They also made small brooms by bundling the shrub's sprigs. They used the brooms for a ritual cleansing, "sweeping" the sickness away.

How Did Shamans Serve as Guides on Non-spiritual Matters?

Many Maya visited the shamans for physical healing or assistance with spiritual things. Yet, the shamans were also known for their insight. If people couldn't resolve problems, such as relationship issues, they might visit a shaman for advice. The Maya kings usually had a group of shamans as their advisors. These shamans used a combination of intuition and knowledge they gained from visions to advise the king on going to war, building a new pyramid, and many other administrative issues.

Roundup Activity: Crossword

Maya Shamans

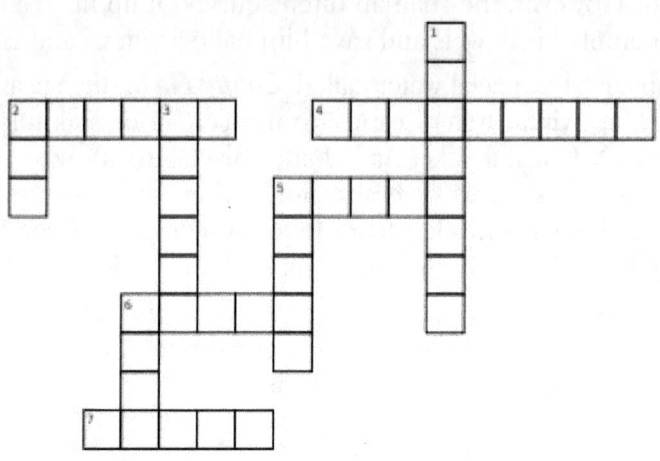

Down:
1. shamans used this to cast out spirits causing sickness
2. an incense made from the Copal tree
3. an altered state of consciousness
5. an emblem representing the sacred Ceiba tree
6. a small gourd the Maya used to drink balché

Across:
2. a cactus with hallucinogenic growths
4. secretions of the cane toad
5. shamans performed ceremonies asking this god to send rain
6. shamans made medicine from this
7. clay figurines shamans called on

Image source[48]

Chapter 9: Maya Mysteries and Magical Folktales

Ancient Maya folklore has many enchanting stories, and this chapter will unwrap a few. But first, let's investigate a mesmerizing mystery. It involves puzzling artifacts associated with the Maya: the crystal skulls.

The Captivating Mystery of the Crystal Skulls

These mysterious skulls have intrigued historians, archaeologists, and Maya enthusiasts for over a century. Did they possess mystical powers? Who carved them and how? Why do skeptical scholars so hotly debate their authenticity? Let's find out!

It all started with Eugène Boban, the official archaeologist for Maximilian I of Mexico, the Austrian archduke who ruled Mexico in the 1860s. Boban collected Mexican artwork and artifacts. In 1887, he sold a life-sized crystal skull carved from a single block of transparent quartz to an American entrepreneur, George Sisson. Boban said it was from Mexico and ancient but didn't provide other details. Ten years later, the skull made its way to the British Museum. Three other crystal skulls passed from Boban to the Trocadéro Museum in Paris.

Two decades later, another crystal skull showed up. Anna Mitchell-Hedges, daughter of a famous British adventurer and author, said she found it in the ruins of the ancient Maya city of Lubaantun in Belize. Her father claimed it was thousands of years old and had been used by a Maya high priest in rituals to place a death curse on people. Anna went on tour with the skull, charging admission to see it.

Legends cropped up about the skulls, and eventually, around a dozen were floating around Europe and the United States. Supposedly, they had magical powers to heal and transmit ancient wisdom, energy, and information. New Age mythology claimed the ancient Maya had thirteen crystal skulls that could save the Earth if they were all brought together. Skeptics pointed out that the Maya and Aztecs didn't have the technology to craft the skulls. Yet, the New Agers were adamant, suggesting they must be even more ancient than the Maya, made by the lost civilization of Atlantis.

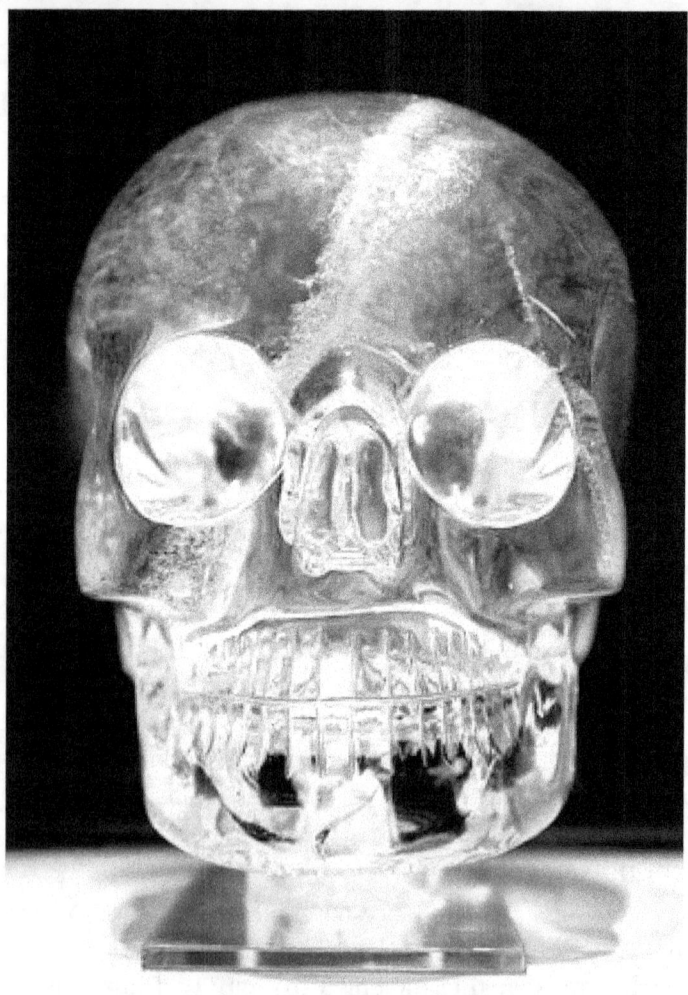

The crystal skull in the British Museum⁴⁹

The buzz swirling around the skulls was so strong that researchers decided to take a closer look at the British Museum skull and another at the Smithsonian Institution. Ancient Mesoamericans did work with crystal. For instance, the Mixtecs of ancient Mexico carved a goblet and beads from rock crystal. Mesoamerica has quartz, but not the type of quartz used for the skulls. Geologists determined that the quartz from which the skulls were carved came from Brazil (or maybe Madagascar), not Mesoamerica. However, Brazil didn't mine quartz until the 1800s, so the ancient Maya wouldn't have had access to it. Moreover, no evidence exists of trade relationships between Brazil and Mesoamerica in ancient times.

Another problem was the carving skills used on the skulls. When examined under a microscope, specialists concluded that the teeth could have only been engraved with a rotary disk tool used by modern jewelers. They discovered the British Museum skull had traces of a synthetic abrasive called carborundum, which was only used in modern times. The skulls were fakes. They weren't made in ancient times by the Maya or anyone else. Using Brazilian quartz, craftspeople in Germany almost certainly carved these two skulls and probably the others that were "discovered" in the late 1800s and early 1900s.

Of the dozen or so skulls, none came from any known archaeological digs. They just mysteriously appeared in Europe or the United States. Yes, Anna Mitchell-Hedges did claim that hers came from a specific dig. Yet, none of the archaeologists at that site ever mentioned the skull. A find that amazing would have been well-documented. The Maya most likely never produced crystal skulls.

However, the Maya did carve breathtaking death masks of turquoise, jade, obsidian, and other valuable rock. The Maya considered these elaborate masterpieces highly sacred. Jade represented the breath of life and rebirth. The masks represented the maize god, who died and resurrected. The jade mask of King Yuknoom Yich'aak K'ahk' at Calakmul has a butterfly under the chin, a sign of metamorphosis. The king died in 698 CE, so the mask is over 1,300 years old.

Jade death mask from Calakmul[50]

Pyramid Magic

The architecture of the Maya pyramids is mind-blowing. The Maya did not have beasts of burden, nor did they have the wheel. They may have known about the wheel because Teotihuacan had children's ceramic toys with wheels and axles. However, no civilization in Mesoamerica appeared to use the wheel functionally for work. They hauled twenty-ton limestone blocks to build their pyramids and other grand structures without the wheel or a pulley system. Some of their pyramids were as high as a twenty-story building. How did they do that?

Today's Maya in Guatemala claim their ancestors did it by whistling! They said their ancestors would whistle a tune, and the big stones and logs would float through the air. Using different tunes, the whistler would give the stones and logs directions for where to go. However, one day, someone offended the gods by using tools. After this, the stone and logs no longer obeyed the whistles.

Undoubtedly, the modern-day Maya were having fun with the tourists with this story. Yet, one Maya pyramid really does chirp like a bird! The El Castillo pyramid at Chichén Itzá is an acoustic engineering masterpiece. As you may remember, it's the temple to Kukulkan, who was part serpent and part quetzal bird. If one claps loudly in front of El Castillo, the echo sounds just like the quetzal bird's plaintive chirp. But that's not all! When one claps at El Castillo, the bird squawk echo bounces off a nearby temple, making the soft rattle of the serpent.

The serpent's head with El Castillo in the background[51]

The Aluxo'ob, the Leprechauns of Yucatán

When the ancient Maya heard a strange sound at night, they'd say, "It's an alux!" These mythological beings were like leprechauns. They could bring good luck, but if someone offended them, watch out! They could make people sick. Most of the time, aluxo'ob (plural for alux) were invisible. If a person saw one, it was the size of a preschooler, with the wrinkled face of an older man. Aluxo'ob hated change, so if the Maya moved into a new house, they had to honor the aluxo'ob who lived in the region.

Ceramic figurine of an alux[59]

The Maya were a little scared of aluxo'ob. Still, they appreciated how aluxo'ob helped them be wise stewards of nature. If humans failed to protect and conserve nature, they would have a rough time in Xibalba. Aluxo'ob were the protectors of fields. The Maya farmers would build a little house for them in their maize fields. Aluxo'ob chased away the rats, rabbits, and deer that would eat the corn and negotiated with Chaac for plenty of rain. However, the amicable relationship between a farmer and an alux living on his land went sour at the end of seven years. That's when the alux turned into a maniac and wreaked havoc on the farmland, so the farmer had to seal the alux inside his miniature house.

Xtabay, the Warped Ghost

This Yucatán legend says two beautiful young women once lived in a village. Xkeban had many lovers, which the Maya frowned upon. Yet, she generously helped the poor and disabled and was kind to animals. Utz-Colel was sexually pure yet cold-hearted and proud. She never did anything to help another person, much less an animal. She was often cruel and scorned the people suffering from poverty or disability.

One day, Xkeban died. The poor people in the village held a funeral for her, and the animals guarded her grave. She reincarnated as a purple morning glory that grew around her gravesite, filling the air with a sweet scent. Years later, Utz-Colel died, but the only thing that grew from her grave was the smelly Tzacam cactus. She begged the Lords of Death, "Bring me back to life so I can get another chance to become a beautiful flower when I die the next time."

The gods reincarnated her, not as a woman but as a demon named Xtabay. She appeared like a lovely young woman with shiny black hair reaching her ankles and beautiful large black eyes, yet she was a predator. She lurked under a ceiba tree, waiting for men to walk through the forest at night. She enticed them to have sex with her to their great peril. Some of her victims got lost in the forest and never found their way out again. Occasionally, she turned herself into a giant snake and ate her lover. Other times, she pushed them off a cliff or ripped out their hearts. The story's moral is that the gods considered pride and cruelty worse than sexual immorality. Kindness and generosity to the helpless were all-important virtues.

A Lethal Battle for Love

Two warrior princes lived in the Yucatán jungle of Quintana Roo. Kinich was the younger brother and was considerate and helpful to everyone. His older brother, Tizic, was arrogant and lacked compassion. One day, they met a lovely young woman named Nicté-Ha. She was a gentle soul, beautiful inside and out. Both brothers fell in love with her and wanted to marry her.

As previously mentioned, love matches weren't a Maya thing. The matchmaker and parents were supposed to arrange marriages. Yet, both brothers ignored convention. They didn't even ask Nicté-Ha whom she preferred. Instead, they decided to fight to the death that night. The last man standing would marry the stunning maiden.

The gods were furious with their foolhardy decision. The brothers were ignoring tradition and, worse yet, vowing to kill each other. The gods covered the moon, throwing the jungle night into pitch darkness, trying to stop the battle. Yet, the brothers were unstoppable. They fought fiercely in the black night and killed each other. When they arrived in Xibalba, they desperately petitioned the Lords of Death. "Please! Reincarnate us. We can't bear not being able to see Nicté-Ha!"

"Alright. We'll reincarnate you, but not as men. No more of this foolishness about fighting for her love. Instead, you'll be trees. You can look at her, but that's all."

So, the brothers became trees, growing next to each other. Tizic became a poisonous tree called the Chechén. If his leaves brushed against someone, toxins burned their skin. Kinich became the Chacá tree, which produced an antidote to the Chechén tree's poison. Wherever one sees a Chechén tree in the jungle, a Chacá tree will be nearby. What about Nicté-Ha? When she died, the Lords of Death allowed her to reincarnate as a lovely white lily floating in the cenotes and lagoons.

The Talking Tree

The creator gods placed trees on Earth before creating animals and humans. They made trees for many reasons. Trees produced fruit, nuts, and cacao beans for people and animals to enjoy. Shamans used the leaves and bark of certain trees in herbal medicine. The wood from trees could be used to build houses. People once understood all this and carefully conserved the trees of the jungle.

Yet, as time passed, the humans forgot how helpful the trees were. They felt the trees were in the way, so they began chopping down the great forests. One tree in particular was sad to see all his fellow trees getting cut down. He had once been a joyful tree, lifting his limbs to the heavens. Now, he dejectedly awaited his death. However, as a farmer approached with his axe, the tree suddenly yelled, "Don't cut me!"

The farmer dropped his axe, his face white in fear. "I ... I didn't know trees could talk!"

"We can all speak when we are desperate," the tree replied. "I am Ciri Cote. Did you know that we trees are the connection between Xibalba and the heavens?"

The farmer was still wondering why the tree was speaking. "I don't understand. I cut down other trees. Why didn't they say anything?"

"The trees you cut down before willingly gave you the gift of their wood. We will sacrifice ourselves for a worthy cause."

"I didn't mean to hurt you!" the farmer replied. "But I need this land to grow crops so my family can eat."

"I'm not willing to sacrifice myself," Ciri Cote said. "I have a different purpose. Leave me standing when you plant your corn. You'll soon learn why I'm here!"

So, the farmer left Ciri Cote standing and planted his corn and vegetables nearby. Ciri Cote grew tall, and his spreading limbs produced mouthwatering fruit. The farmer's family and the woodland animals all enjoyed the fruit. They loved resting in Ciri Cote's shade. The farmer and Ciri Cote rejoiced in their friendship, and the farmer learned he could coexist with the animals and trees. Among the animals were rabbits, about whom the Maya had many folk tales.

The Rabbit's Antlers

Curiously, the Maya believed that rabbits originally had antlers. Also, they used to call rabbits "mayor," but the reason is obscure. The Maya told their rabbit stories with music and dance.

Mayor Rabbit was hopping through the forest when he saw Deer. "Look, brother! See the fine cap our Creator Father gave me," he said, pointing to his antlers.

Deer cocked his head. "I think they're too big for you. Those antlers will fit me better. Let me borrow them."

Mayor Rabbit handed his antlers to Deer. "Oh!" said Deer, "These fit perfectly. Look how handsome I am! I'll dance around so you can see."

Deer pranced around Rabbit, then said, "I can't wait to show the others! I'll be right back!"

Deer raced off and never returned. Rabbit waited patiently and then realized Deer had tricked him. He wept bitterly, then decided to see the king.

"My father," said Mayor Rabbit, "Deer stole my antlers! Can you make me a new cap?" And, while you're at it, can you make me bigger? Deer said I was too small!"

"Yes, my son," said the king. "I'll make you bigger. But first, bring me fifteen bundles of skins. Then I'll make you grow and give you your antlers back."

Rabbit ran off, hopping through the fields. On his journey, he bought a guitar. As he was resting and playing his guitar, a snake slithered up. "What are you doing, brother?"

"I'm playing my guitar for you, Uncle," said Mayor Rabbit.

"Your song is sad, but may I dance for you?" asked Uncle Snake.

"Of course!" said Rabbit. "But first, tell me where your weak spot is."

"It's right here, at my tail."

"Then dance away!" said Rabbit.

Snake was unaware that Rabbit was on a secret mission to collect skins for the king. As Snake danced, he came nearer to Rabbit, who killed him and took his skin. Next, Mayor Rabbit hopped up a mountain, where he met Cougar.

"Would you like me to play some music, Uncle Cougar?"

"Oh yes! Play some dancing music! I love to dance!"

"Okay. Just tell me your weak spot!"

"Here it is," answered Cougar, "on the back of my neck."

So, Rabbit played, and Cougar danced. But Cougar got too close, and Rabbit knocked him with a log in his weak spot, killing him and collecting his skin. Next, Rabbit hopped to the beach and played his guitar. An alligator crawled up. "I love your music! Can I dance?"

"Of course! Just show me your weak spot so I don't accidentally bump it."

"It's here, at the end of my tail," answered the alligator. He began dancing, but Rabbit killed and skinned him, too. His bags were getting full of skins.

Next, Mayor Rabbit hopped to a plantation where guava and avocados grew. He picked some guava and hopped to the house where the monkeys lived. "Oh, uncle!" the monkeys said, "Your guava look delicious!"

"Have some!" said Rabbit. "There's a nearby plantation with many more. It has avocados, too!"

"We'd love to go there tomorrow!" the monkeys said. "And, our friends, the coatis, are starving. Can they come too?"

"Of course!" Rabbit said. The next morning, Rabbit took the monkeys and coatis to the plantation. Everyone ate until he could eat no more.

"Make me two nets!" Rabbit commanded.

"Why?"

"I want to see who weighs the most—the monkeys or the coatis!"

Maya ceramic rabbit[58]

"Oh, okay." The monkeys and coatis made the nets and hopped in. But Rabbit hit them all with a club and killed them. He skinned them and put the skins in his bundles. They were now too heavy to carry. So, he got an armadillo to carry his bag for him, and they went to the king.

"Here they are, father! Here are the skins you asked me to bring."

The king was astonished that Mayor Rabbit had killed so many animals. He never expected he'd be able to do it.

"Now make me big and give me my antlers back!" Rabbit demanded.

"But Rabbit! Even though you're small, you killed all these animals!" the king cried. "If I make you bigger, you'd kill everyone. I can't do that! Nor will I give you the antlers back. Instead, I'll stretch out your ears. Come here!"

So, Rabbit hopped up to the throne, and the king stretched out his ears. That's why rabbits have long ears today.

Roundup Activity: Short Answer

1. What are at least three reasons the Maya did NOT carve the crystal skulls?

2. Why was jade a favorite stone for death masks?

3. What sound does El Castillo make if you clap loudly in front of it?

4. How did the aluxo'ob protect the fields?

5. What did the Maya gods consider worse than sexual immorality? What were essential virtues?

6. After Kinich and Tizic killed each other, what did they become when reincarnated?

7. Why was the farmer glad he didn't cut down Ciri Cote, the tree?

8. Who stole Mayor Rabbit's antlers?

Chapter 10: More Exciting Exploits of the Hero Twins

We've already unwrapped the Hero Twins' famous ball game in Xibalba when they defeated the Lords of Death. But what other adventures did they have as children and young teens? This chapter unlocks several myths from the *Popol Vuh* of their rollicking escapades before they upended the underworld.

Hunahpu and Xbalanque at Grandmother Xmucane's House

This story begins after the twins' mother, Xquic, escapes from Xibalba. She is pregnant with the boys after their father, Hunahpu One, spits on her hand. His mother, Xmucane, has grudgingly agreed to let Xquic live with her. After giving birth, Xquic names her twins Hunahpu and Xbalanque. Xquic disappears from the *Popol Vuh* narrative at this time. (Later, the twins call themselves "orphans," so perhaps she died.)

Her babies are fussy at their grandmother's house, refusing to sleep. Xmucane isn't very grandmotherly.

"I can't stand their shrill crying!" Xmucane wails. "Take them out and abandon them!"

Their older half-brothers, the Monkey Twins, are jealous. They don't want competition from their younger half-brothers, who are famous for their wisdom, musical talent, writings, and carvings. They take the babies out and put them on an anthill. The babies fall peacefully asleep, and the ants don't sting them. The Monkey Twins then put them on a thornbush and leave them there.

The younger twins learn how to fend for themselves as babies. Fortunately, they are gods, so they manage to find food. They learn to kill birds with their blowguns, yet the Monkey Twins steal the birds from them.

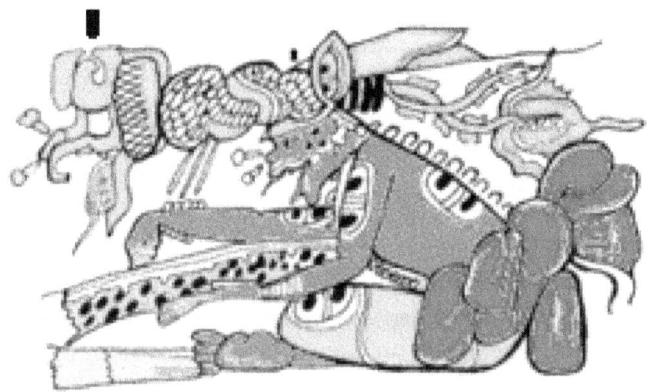

Hun Batz Hun Cheuén
Monkey Artist Gods

One of the Monkey Twins"

One day, Hunahpu and Xbalanque come home with no birds. Grandmother Xmucane angrily asks, "Why didn't you bring any birds home?"

"Grandmother, we shoot them, but they get stuck in the top of the tree. We're too small to climb up there. Maybe our older brothers could help us."

The Monkey Twins agree to help, so they go into the jungle to a high tree full of birds, riotously singing. The Hero Twins shoot the birds, but none fall to the ground. So, the Monkey Twins climb the tree to get the birds stuck in the branches. However, as they climb, the tree swells and grows taller. The Monkey Twins call to their brothers, "Help! We're stuck up here!"

"Untie your loincloths and tie them around your hips so the long end hangs behind you. That will give you more freedom to move."

When the Monkey Twins do that, the long piece of loincloth on each young man immediately turns into a monkey tail. Now, they look like spider monkeys. The Hero Twins have used their superpowers to transform their older brothers. From that time on, the Monkey Twins live on the top of the rainforest trees, screeching and chattering.

The younger boys return home. "Grandmother, our older brothers have monkey faces now. They're in the treetops."

"What have you done to them?"

"Please don't cry, Grandmother. They'll be fine."

One boy plays "Hunahpu Spider Monkey" on the flute, and the other pounds on a drum. They call their brothers' names, and Grandmother Xmucane joins in. The Monkey Twins come dancing in, and Grandmother breaks into laughter when she sees their comical monkey faces. The Monkey Twins run off back to the trees.

"Let's try again, but try not to laugh this time, Grandmother."

They call them in again, but Grandmother can't help herself. She roars with laughter, and the Monkey Twins flee, never to return.

"Don't be sad, Grandmother. We're still here. We will remember our older brothers."

Zipacna and the Four Hundred Boys

Seven Macaw, the proud god who falsely said he was the sun, has died. Yet, his two equally prideful sons, Zipacna and Cabracan, are still alive. The Maya portrayed them as caimans or crocodiles. If you recall, Zipacna was the one who bragged that he created the mountains. His pride and violence are his doom.

Zipacna (Cipactli in Nahuatl) from the Codex Magliabechiano"

One day, Zipacna is swimming in a river when four hundred boys approach, dragging an enormous tree.

"What are you boys doing?" Zipacna asks.

"We just cut down this tree," the boys explain. "But it's so heavy we can only drag it. We can't lift it on our shoulders."

"Let me help!" Zipacna volunteers, and he throws the tree on his back. "What are you planning to do with this tree?"

"It will be the support beam for the house we're building."

"I see," Zipacna says. "Well, lead the way."

He follows the boys to the house they are building and sets the tree down.

"Thank you so much!" the boys say, gathering around. "Why don't you spend the night with us? Or do you live with your parents?"

"No," Zipacna sadly answers. "They both died recently."

"Oh, we are sorry to hear that," the four hundred boys respond. "Stay with us! We're planning to erect the beam tomorrow. You can help us!"

Zipacna agrees to stay with the four hundred boys. But after he falls asleep, the boys make devious plans. "That stranger is too strong! All four hundred of us could only drag that tree, but he lifted it on his back with no problem. What would he do to us if he got angry?"

"We need to kill him! But how? He's so strong!"

"I know!" says one boy. "We'll ask him to help us dig the hole for the support beam. Then, when he's at the bottom, we'll throw the tree and dirt in on top of him!"

So, the next morning, the boys start digging the hole. After a while, they call for Zipacna. "We're digging this hole for the support beam, but this is as deep as we can go. Can you finish digging it for us?"

"Of course!" Zipacna jumps into the hole.

"It needs to be really deep to hold the tree up!" the boys tell him. "Call us when you're finished."

However, Zipacna had figured out the boys' evil plan. He had already dug a tunnel under the house to the hole. After jumping in, he quickly digs to the side, giving him access to his tunnel.

"How far down are you now?" the boys ask.

"I'm done!" he calls up. But Zipacna isn't in the hole; he's in the connecting tunnel. When the boys throw the tree down, it doesn't hurt him. Yet, he screams to trick the boys.

"Good! He's dead now!" the boys say. "Let's make balché and drink! After he begins decomposing, we'll see the ants coming out with his body pieces. We'll know for sure he's dead then."

The boys spend the next three days getting thoroughly drunk. Then, they see the ants crawling out of the hole with bits of hair and fingernails.

"Look! The ants are eating his body! He's really dead. Let's drink to our success!"

Yet, Zipacna is very much alive. He had just cut some of his hair and nails to feed the ants. Then, he passed through his tunnel and went outside. Now, he is atop the boys' house while they lie inside drunk. He crushes the house, killing all the boys inside. They become the four hundred stars of Wakaxo', the constellation of the bull.

The Hero Twins (possibly Zipacna in the center) from a Maya vase[66]

Zipacna and the Twins

When the twin gods, Hunahpu and Xbalanque, hear that Zipacna has killed the four hundred boys, they vow revenge. Zipacna spends his days along the rivers, looking for fish and crabs to eat. At night, he carries mountains around on his back. The twins make a fake crab, using a stone for its body and bromeliad blossoms for its claws. They place the fake crab at the bottom of a cave in the depths of Mount Meauan. Then, they go looking for Zipacna, who doesn't know them and isn't aware of the part they played in his father's death.

The twins find Zipacna at a riverside. "What are you doing?" they ask.

"I'm looking for something to eat! I only eat fish and crabs, yet I haven't found any in two days. I'm starving!"

"Oh!" the twins answer. "We just saw a huge crab in the cave under Mount Meauan. We tried to catch it, but it pinched us with its enormous claws. Maybe you'll have better luck."

"Will you take me there?" Zipacna asks.

"Oh, it will be easy to find. Just follow the river to Mount Meauan. He's down in that cave where the river flows from under the mountain."

"Please guide me! If you do, I'll show you where some birds are that you can shoot with your blowguns," Zipacna begs.

So, the twins lead Zipacna to the cave under the mountain and point to the fake crab, "There it is!"

The cave entrance is tight, but Zipacna crawls in after the crab. The twins pull a string, and the crab appears to scuttle out of the water and up the cave wall. Zipacna pushes himself back out.

"Did you catch the crab?" the twins ask.

"No! He went up the cave wall. I will turn over and go in on my back to get to him."

Zipacna pushes himself in until only his rear legs and tail hang out. Suddenly, the mountain settles on top of him, turning him into stone. The boys had used their enchantment to entrap him.

The Twins Defeat Cabracan

Seven Macaw's other prideful son, Cabracan (Kab'raqan), brags that he is the "Wrecker of Mountains." (His name is the K'iche' word for "earthquake.") The creator god, Hurricane, visits the twins.

"I command you to defeat Seven Macaw's other son. These boys have caused trouble on the earth. They believe they are greater than the sun! Their pride is out of place. Lure him to the east, where the sun rises."

"Very well, Hurricane, Heart of the Sky. Yes, we also disapprove of his pride."

Maya mask, probably Hurricane[57]

The twins go looking for Cabracan and find him tipping mountains over.

"Where are you going?" they ask.

"I'm not going anywhere. Look! All I have to do is tap my foot on the ground, and the mountains tumble over. I can do this all day!" Cabracan brags. "Who are you? I haven't seen you around before."

The twins humbly answer, "We're nobody special. We don't even have names. We're just poor orphans who kill birds with our blowguns to eat. But we just saw a gigantic mountain that keeps growing. It's higher than all the other mountains. It was too high for us to climb up to catch birds. Can you really make mountains fall?"

"Take me to that mountain!" Cabracan insists. "I'll show you how I can level it!"

"It's in the east, where the sun rises. We'll take you there and shoot some birds with our blowguns on the way."

So, they set off. The twins use their blowguns to kill some birds. Cabracan is surprised to see the boys don't have any pellets in their blowguns; they're just blowing air. The twins make a fire to cook the birds but cover one of the birds with quicklime. Cabracan's mouth waters at the smell of the roasting birds.

"What's that you're eating? It smells delicious! Give me a little."

The boys give him the bird with the lime on it. Then, they get up and continue their journey. However, Cabracan's arms and legs are weak after eating the lime. He can't make the majestic mountain fall. He can't defend himself when the twins tie him up and bury him. That is the end of Cabracan.

Maya stone reptile, possibly Cabracan[58]

The Hero Twins and the Rat in the Cornfield

"Grandmother!" say the Hero Twins, Hunahpu and Xbalanque. "We're going to go out and farm the cornfield. Can you bring us our lunch later?"

"Yes, my grandsons," answers Xmucane.

The brothers set off, carrying their hoe, axe, and blowguns. They set the hoe in the ground when they get to the cornfield. Under their enchantment, the hoe moves by itself, clearing out the briars and old cornstalks. The boys want to enlarge the field, which means chopping down a stand of trees. All they do is place the axe in the fork of a tree, and it goes to work, busily chopping down the trees by itself.

A turtle dove is cooing nearby. The twins place him on a large stump. "Keep an eye out for our grandmother. When you see her coming, coo loudly!"

Since the hoe and axe do all the work, the boys spend their morning hunting birds with their blowguns. When the dove calls them, they hurry back to the field and grab the hoe and axe. They rub dirt on their faces and throw wood chips in their hair to make their grandmother think they've worked hard in the field. Grandmother Xmucane brings them their lunch, looking around proudly at how much work has been done.

That evening, they drag themselves into the house, pretending to be exhausted. "We're so tired, Grandmother!" They rub their arms and thighs as if their muscles are sore.

The following day, the brothers head back out to the field. But then, they almost fall down in surprise. The trees and briars are all back!

"Someone's playing a trick on us! But who? And how?"

A coalition of the woodland animals had put everything back. It was the birds, the coati, the coyote, the deer, the fox, the jaguar, the peccary, the puma, the rabbit, and the rat.

So, the boys get back to work. That is, their hoe and axe work while they hunt again. When evening approaches, they discuss their plan. "We'll come back out here tonight and guard the field. Then we'll find out who did the mischief last night."

After eating supper, they return to the field and hide in the edge of the woods. The animals gather again in the middle of the night, chirping, growling, and chattering. They command the briars and trees: "Arise!"

The boys look on in astonishment as the animals pass their hiding spot. The first two are the jaguar and puma. The boys try to catch them, but they are too strong and swift. Next come the deer and rabbit. The boys grab their tails, but they fall off, and the animals run away. That's why deer and rabbits have short tails today. The coati, the coyote, the fox, and the peccary run off before the boys can get them.

Then, along comes a rat. The boys catch him in a net. They hold his tail over a fire, which is why rats have bare tails now. But the rat squeaks out, "You must not kill me! I know something that belongs to you!"

"What is it?" ask the twins.

"Let me go and give me a little food. Then I'll tell you."

"We'll feed you later," say the twins. "Tell us now!"

"Oh, alright," says the rat. "It's something that belonged to your father and uncle. They left their ball and ball game equipment at your grandmother's house, hidden in the rafters."

"Really?!" The twins are overjoyed.

"Here! Have some corn!" the boys say. "Here are some beans, chocolate, squash seeds, and chili peppers. You can come live at our house, and we'll give you the leftovers and food that drops to the floor."

"Sounds great!" the rat says happily. He goes with the boys and shows them where their father hid his rubber ball and game equipment. That's what led to their eventual ball game in Xibalba.

Roundup Activity: Who Am I?

Choose the correct answer for each description from the list below. Check your answers in the back of the book.

Cabracan	Hurricane	Monkey Twins
the rat	Xmucane	Xquic	Zipacna

_____ 1. I was the Hero Twins' mother.

_____ 2. I was the Hero Twins' grandmother.

_____ 3. We were the Hero Twins' older half-brothers.

_____ 4. I was Seven Macaw's son and killed the 400 boys.

_____ 5. I commanded the Hero Twins to kill Cabracan.

_____ 6. I was Zipacna's son and Cabracan's brother.

_____ 7. I showed the twins where their father's ball was.

Answers to Roundup Questions

Chapter 1: Comprehension Questions

1. Why did the K'iche' Maya hide the *Popol Vuh* from the Spaniards for two centuries? Who translated it into Spanish?

   To keep the Spaniards from destroying their book of history and culture

2. Who were the two oldest gods in Maya mythology? What other three gods worked with them to create the world and people?

   Grandmother Xmucane, the Maker, and Grandfather Xpiyacoc, the Builder

   Tepew, the Sovereign; Q'ukumatz, the Feathered Serpent; and Huracán, the Hurricane

3. What did the gods use to make humans in their first two unsuccessful tries?

   #1 Mud #2 Wood and reeds

4. What was the sin of Seven Macaw and his sons?

   pride

5. What did the gods finally use to create humans successfully?

   Corn flour dough

6. What problem did the people have after they were created?

   No sun

7. What god told the K'iche' people to sacrifice human hearts?
Tohil

Chapter 2: Who Am I?
1. I was a creator god who taught the humans about writing, medicine, and law. **Kukulkan**
2. I was the droopy-nosed, fanged rain god. **Chaac**
3. I was the Face of the Sun and the god of healing. **K'inich Ahau**
4. I was the supreme god of the sky. **Itzamná**
5. I was the moon goddess and wife of Itzamná. **Ixchel**
6. I was Ixchel's son and god of nature. **Yum Kaax**
7. I was the bad god of violence and war. **Buluc-Chabtan**
8. I ruled Xibalba, the underworld. **Ah Puch**
9. We were bat demons who ate people's heads. **Camazotz**
10. We stabbed people who didn't take out the trash or keep their yards clean. **Sweeping Demon and Stabbing Demon**

Chapter 3: When Did It Happen?
(10) A bat cuts off Hunahpu's head.
(8) A mosquito helps the Hero Twins, Hunahpu and Xbalanque, in Xibalba.
(12) Hunahpu and Xbalanque defeat the Lords of Death.
(3) One Hunahpu and Seven Hunahpu sit on a burning hot rock that scorches their bottoms.
(1) One Hunahpu's wife, Xbaquiyalo, gives birth to the Monkey Twins.
(5) Princess Xquic gets pregnant from One Hunahpu's spit.
(7) The Hero Twins discover their father's old ball court.
(9) The Hero Twins lose the first round of the ball game.
(2) The Lords of Death command One Hunahpu and Seven Hunahpu to play ball in Xibalba.
(4) The Lords of Death sacrifice One Hunahpu and Seven Hunahpu.
(6) The owls help Xquic escape from being sacrificed.

(11) Xbalanque replaces Hunahpu's head with a round squash.

Chapter 4: True or False?

1. (F) The god Hunahpu introduced the calendar to humans.
2. (T) The Tzolk'in was the Maya religious or festival calendar.
3. (F) The Maya had lunar months of about 30 days.
4. (T) The Calendar Round coordinated the solar and festival calendars.
5. (T) The Maya date of creation was 3114 BCE.
6. (T) 2012 CE was when a new Long Count cycle began for the Maya.
7. (T) El Caracol at Chichén Itzá was an observatory to track Venus's cycles.
8. (F) The Maya "star wars" involved competition between Saturn and the sun.
9. (T) Aguada Fénix lined up with the sunrise on a zenith day.
10. (T) Many early Maya cities aligned with the sunrise on two dates 260 days apart.

Chapter 5: Multiple Choice

1. The first writers in North America were:
   c. The Olmecs
2. How many glyphs are on the Cascajal Block?
   c. 62
3. What did the Zapotec glyphs between a sacrificial victim's legs read?
   a. Earthquake
4. Where were the first known Maya glyphs found?
   c. San Bartolo
5. What part of the Maya logo-syllabic script represented whole words, like water or mountain?
   a. Logograms

6. What were the smaller parts of a glyph that changed the word, such as making it plural or in the past tense?
   a. Affixes
7. How did the Maya usually read their hieroglyphics?
   c. Horizontally for two glyphs and then down to the next row
8. Who cracked the code to Maya numerals in 1832?
   d. Rafinesque
9. What teenager made a stunning breakthrough in reading Maya glyphs in the 1980s?
   b. David Stuart

Chapter 6: Comprehension Questions

1. How did the layout and architecture of Tikal reflect Maya cosmology and religious beliefs?

   The towering Tikal pyramids may have symbolized the connection between the earthly realm and the heavens. The many pyramids in Tikal were related to the Maya religious calendar. In the late 600s CE, the Maya began building a new twin pyramid complex each "k'atun," or every twenty years.

2. Why was Tikal's location considered spiritually significant to the ancient Maya?

   The "Yax Che" (ceiba or kapok) trees dominated the rainforests around Tikal. The Maya thought the kapok was the "World Tree," the portal between heaven, Earth, and the underworld. The Lost World temple area was an "E-Group" astronomical complex, marking sunrises on March 11 and October 2.

3. How did the Teotihuacanos influence Maya temples?

   Tikal had a temple complex that was a miniature copy of Teotihuacan's Citadel. Green obsidian glass from Teotihuacan decorated the Tikal complex. The Tikal temple was oriented fifteen degrees east of true north, remarkably similar to the Citadel at Teotihuacan.

4. What Maya myth was inscribed on human bones in Sky Rain's tomb?

"*Crossing the Milky Way in the Cosmic Canoe.*" *The other gods mourn the dead maize god (One Hunahpu) as they paddle the cosmic canoe carrying the dead god across the Milky Way to the center of the cosmos.*

5. Around what beliefs did Maya prayers and rituals revolve?

Around their belief that they were sinful and the forces of the universe determined their fate. They humbly approached the gods, knowing their deities could give them good or bad fortune. If the Maya wanted to build a house or go on a hunting expedition, they would consult their priests about when to start.

Chapter 7: Fill in the Blank

The Maya cosmology was **dualistic**, meaning they saw things as pairs or parallel. The **Hetzmek** ceremony marked the "breaking the baby's legs," when instead of being swaddled, he or she was carried straddling the mother's hip. A Maya teen boy had to go through a **bloodletting** ritual as part of his coming-of-age ceremony. A **matchmaker** arranged the marriage of a young Maya couple. **Humul** dancers wore big racks with feathers on their backs and portrayed Maya myths. The Maya believed almost everyone went to **Xibalba** when they died, although they might later be reincarnated. The only way to get into Maya heaven was to die a **violent** death. Most Maya buried their family members under their **house**. The Maya sprinkled **cinnabar** on their dead nobles, believing it reanimated the dead.

Chapter 8: Crossword

Maya Shamans

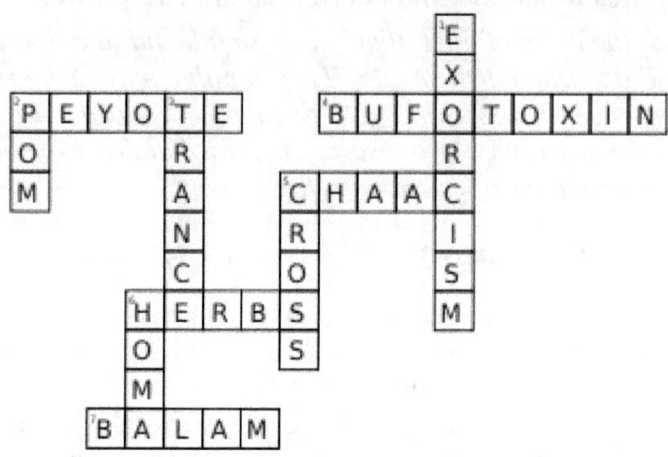

Down:
1. shamans used this to cast out spirits causing sickness
2. an incense made from the Copal tree
3. an altered state of consciousness
5. an emblem representing the sacred Ceiba tree
6. a small gourd the Maya used to drink balché

Across:
2. a cactus with hallucinogenic growths
4. secretions of the cane toad
5. shamans performed ceremonies asking this god to send rain
6. shamans made medicine from this
7. clay figurines shamans called on

Image source[89]

Chapter 9: Short Answer

1. What were at least three reasons the Maya did NOT carve the crystal skulls?
   - They didn't have the technical ability.
   - The quartz came from Brazil, not Mesoamerica.
   - The teeth were engraved with a modern rotary disk tool.
   - The British skull had traces of a modern synthetic abrasive called carborundum.
   - None of the skulls were verified to have come from known archaeological digs.

2. Why was jade a favorite stone for death masks?
   Jade represented the breath of life and rebirth.

3. What sound does the El Castillo pyramid make if you clap loudly in front of it?
   The echo sounds like the quetzal bird chirp, followed by a soft rattle.

4. How did the aluxo'ob protect the fields?
   They chased away animals that would eat the corn, like rats, rabbits, and deer.

5. What did the Maya gods consider worse than sexual immorality? What were essential virtues?
   Pride and cruelty. Kindness and generosity to the helpless were all-important virtues.

6. After Kinich and Tizic killed each other, what did they become when reincarnated?
   The Chechén and the Chacá tree. The latter was an antidote to the Chechén tree toxin.

7. Why was the farmer glad he didn't cut down Ciri Cote, the tree?
   It grew delicious fruit, it provided shade, and the farmer became friends with the tree.

8. Who stole Mayor Rabbit's antlers?
   The deer

Chapter 10: Who Am I?

Xquic 1. I was the Hero Twins' mother.

Xmucane 2. I was the Hero Twins' grandmother.

Monkey Twins 3. We were the Hero Twins' older half-brothers.

Zipacna 4. I was Seven Macaw's son and killed the 400 boys.

Hurricane 5. I commanded the Hero Twins to kill Cabracan.

Cabracan 6. I was Zipacna's son and Cabracan's brother.

the rat 7. I showed the twins where their father's ball was.

If you enjoyed this book, a review on Amazon would be greatly appreciated because it would mean a lot to hear from you.

To leave a review:
1. Open your camera app.
2. Point your mobile device at the QR code.
3. The review page will appear in your web browser.

Thanks for your support!

Here's another book by Enthralling History that you might like

Free limited time bonus

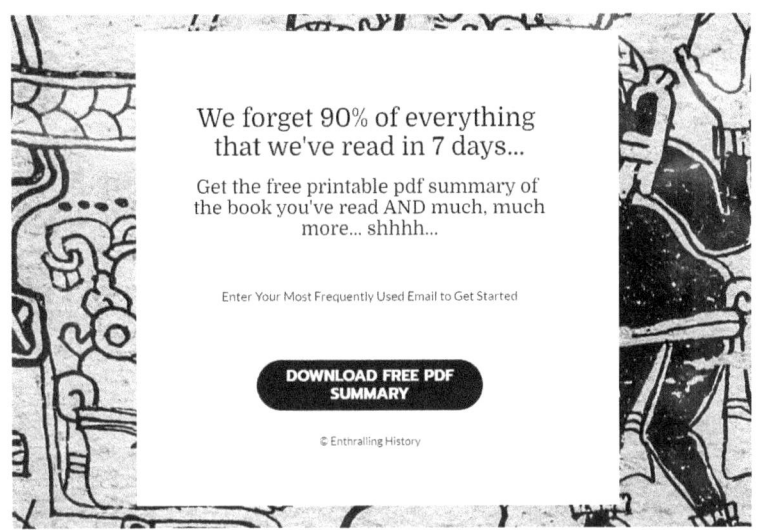

Stop for a moment. We have a free bonus set up for you. The problem is this: we forget 90% of everything that we read after 7 days. Crazy fact, right? Here's the solution: we've created a printable, 1-page pdf summary for this book that you're reading now. All you have to do to get your free pdf summary is to go to the following website: **https://livetolearn.lpages.co/enthrallinghistory/**

Or, Scan the QR code!

Once you do, it will be intuitive. Enjoy, and thank you!

Bibliography

Barquera, R., O. Del Castillo-Chávez, K. Nägele, et al. "Ancient Genomes Reveal Insights into Ritual Life at Chichén Itzá." *Nature* 630 (2024): 912-919. https://doi.org/10.1038/s41586-024-07509-7.

Blomster, J.P., and Chávez Salazar. "Origins of the Mesoamerican Ballgame: Earliest Ballcourt from the Highlands Found at Etlatongo, Oaxaca, Mexico." *Science Advances* 6, no. 11 (March 13, 2020). https://doi.org/10.1126/sciadv.aay6964.

Coe, Michael D. *The Maya (Ancient Peoples and Places Series)*. Thames & Hudson, 1999.

Demarest, Arthur. *Ancient Maya: The Rise and Fall of a Forest Civilization*. Cambridge University Press, 2004.

Evans, Susan T. *Ancient Mexico and Central America: Archaeology and Culture History*. Thames and Hudson, 2004.

Frey, Georges. "The Endless Conquest of Yucatán." *Popular Archaeology*, January 14, 2022. https://popular-archaeology.com/article/the-endless-conquest-of-yucatan/.

Haly, Richard. "Bare Bones: Rethinking Mesoamerican Divinity." *History of Religions* 31, no. 3 (1992): 269-304. http://www.jstor.org/stable/1062864.

Hassig, Ross. *War and Society in Ancient Mesoamerica*. University of California Press, 1992.

Hosler, Dorothy, Sandra Burkett, and Michael Tarkanian. "Prehistoric Polymers: Rubber Processing in Ancient Mesoamerica." *Science* 284, no. 5422 (1988-91). https://doi.org/10.1126/science.284.5422.1988.

Houston, Stephen, and David Stuart. Stuart, David. "Of Gods, Glyphs, and Kings: Divinity and Rulership among the Classic Maya." *Antiquity* 70, no. 268

(1996): 289-312. https://doi.org/10.1017/S0003598X00083289.

Inomata, T, D., F. Triadan, F. Pinzón, and K. Aoyama. "Artificial Plateau Construction during the Preclassic Period at the Maya Site of Ceibal, Guatemala." *PLoS One* 14, no. 8 (2019). https://doi.org/10.1371/journal.pone.0221943.

Jarus, Owen. "Rubber Balls Used in Famous Maya Game Contained Ashes of Cremated Rulers, Archaeologists Claim." *LiveScience: Archaeology*, August 11, 2022. https://www.livescience.com/maya-rubber-balls-cremation.

McVicker, Donald. "The 'Mayanized' Mexicans." *American Antiquity* 50, no. 1 (1985): 82-101. https://doi.org/10.2307/280635.

Popol Vuh: Sacred Book of the Quiché Maya People. Translated by Allen J. Christenson. University of Oklahoma Press, 2007. https://www.mesoweb.com/publications/Christenson/PopolVuh.pdf.

Sabloff, Jeremy A. "It Depends on How We Look at Things: New Perspectives on the Postclassic Period in the Northern Maya Lowlands." *Proceedings of the American Philosophical Society* 151, no. 1 (2007): 11-26. http://www.jstor.org/stable/4599041.

Sahagún, Fray Bernardino de. *Historia General de las Cosas de Nueva España*. Edited by Francisco del Paso y Troncoso. Fototipia de Hauser y Menet, 1905.

Saturno, William A., David Stuart, and Boris Beltrán. "Early Maya Writing at San Bartolo, Guatemala." *Science*, March 3, 2006. https://www.science.org/doi/10.1126/science.1121745?ijkey=SvObjuiMMdrVY&keytype=ref&siteid=sci.

Shook, Edwin M., and Alfred V. Kidder. "Mound E-III-3, K'aminaljuyu, Guatemala." In *Contributions to American Anthropology and History* 9, no. 53 (1952): 33-127. Carnegie Institution of Washington.

Spence, Lewis. *The Myths of Mexico and Peru*. George Harrap, 1913. https://www.sacred-texts.com/nam/mmp/index.htm.

Sprajc, Ivan, Takeshi Inomata, and Anthony F. Aveni. "Origins of Mesoamerican Astronomy and Calendar: Evidence from the Olmec and Maya Regions." *Science Advances* 9, no. 1 (2023). https://www.science.org/doi/10.1126/sciadv.abq7675.

Stuart, David. "Some Working Notes on the Text of Tikal Stela 31." University of Texas, 2011. https://www.mesoweb.com/stuart/notes/Tikal.pdf.

Trik, Aubrey S. "The Splendid Tomb of Temple I at Tikal, Guatemala." *Expedition Magazine* 6, no. 1 (1963). https://www.penn.museum/sites/expedition/the-splendid-tomb-of-temple-i-at-tikal-guatemala/.

Vogt, Evon Zartman. *Tortillas for the Gods: A Symbolic Analysis of Zinacanteco Rituals*. University of Oklahoma Press, 1976.

Image Sources

[1] *Photo Modified: labels added. Nepenthes (converted to English by Kaldari), CC BY-SA 3.0 <https://creativecommons.org/licenses/by-sa/3.0>, via Wikimedia Commons https://commons.wikimedia.org/wiki/File:Maya_region_w_german_names.png*

[2] *Photo zoomed in. Daniel Schwen, CC BY-SA 4.0 <https://creativecommons.org/licenses/by-sa/4.0>, via Wikimedia Commons: https://commons.wikimedia.org/wiki/File:Chichen_Itza_3.jpg*

[3] *Photo zoomed in. Xjunajpù, CC BY-SA 3.0 <https://creativecommons.org/licenses/by-sa/3.0>, via Wikimedia Commons: https://commons.wikimedia.org/wiki/File:Popol_Wuj%27s_deity.png*

[4] *https://commons.wikimedia.org/wiki/File:YaxchilanDivineSerpent.jpg#file*

[5] *Photo zoomed in. Xjunajpù, CC BY-SA 3.0 <https://creativecommons.org/licenses/by-sa/3.0>, via Wikimedia Commons: https://commons.wikimedia.org/wiki/File:Popol_Wuj%27s_deity.png*

[6] *Photo zoomed in. CC BY-SA 3.0 <http://creativecommons.org/licenses/by-sa/3.0/>, via Wikimedia Commons: https://commons.wikimedia.org/wiki/File:Toltec-style_Vessel_1.jpg*

[7] *Musée du quai Branly, CC0, via Wikimedia Commons: https://commons.wikimedia.org/wiki/File:Serpent_%C3%A0_plumes_Chichen_Itza.jpg*

[8] *Credit: Gary Todd, CC0, via Wikimedia Commons; https://commons.wikimedia.org/wiki/File:Chaak_Vessel,_Mayapan,_Post_Classic,_1250-1450_AD.jpg*

[9] *Public Domain via Wikimedia Commons: https://commons.wikimedia.org/wiki/File:God_G_Kinich_Ahau_2.jpg*

[10] *Photo zoomed in. https://commons.wikimedia.org/wiki/File:God_D_Itzamna.jpg*

[11] *Photo zoomed in. Lacambalam, CC BY-SA 4.0 <https://creativecommons.org/licenses/by-sa/4.0>, via Wikimedia Commons: https://commons.wikimedia.org/wiki/File:Codex_dresdensis_lacambalam_itzamn%C3%A1.jpg*

[12] *https://commons.wikimedia.org/wiki/File:Ixchel_Dresden.jpg*

[13] Photo by Jay Galvin- Drawing Yum Kax Mayan Nature God, Pilsen, Chicago, CC BY 2.0 <https://creativecommons.org/licenses/by/2.0>, via Wikimedia Commons: https://commons.wikimedia.org/wiki/File:Drawing_Yum_Kaax-_God_of_Wild_Plants_%26_Animals.jpg

[14] Sylvanus Griswold Morley, (1883-1948), Public domain, via Wikimedia Commons: https://commons.wikimedia.org/wiki/File:Maya_Hieroglyphs_Fig_04.jpg

[15] Dennis Jarvis from Halifax, Canada, CC BY-SA 2.0 <https://creativecommons.org/licenses/by-sa/2.0>, via Wikimedia Commons: https://commons.wikimedia.org/wiki/File:Honduras-0334_(2213598531).jpg

[16] Photo zoomed in. Xjunajpù, CC BY-SA 3.0 <https://creativecommons.org/licenses/by-sa/3.0>, via Wikimedia Commons: https://commons.wikimedia.org/wiki/File:Popol_Wuj%27s_deity.png

[17] Kåre Thor Olsen, CC BY-SA 2.5 <https://creativecommons.org/licenses/by-sa/2.5>, via Wikimedia Commons; https://commons.wikimedia.org/wiki/File:Chich%C3%A9n_Itz%C3%A1_Goal.jpg

[18] Toyotsu, CC BY-SA 4.0 <https://creativecommons.org/licenses/by-sa/4.0>, via Wikimedia Commons: https://commons.wikimedia.org/wiki/File:BallGamePlayerFigurine.jpg

[19] Popol Vuh Museum: Simon Burchell, CC BY-SA 4.0 <https://creativecommons.org/licenses/by-sa/4.0>, via Wikimedia Commons: https://commons.wikimedia.org/wiki/File:Museo_Popul_Vuh_161.jpg

[20] Photo zoomed in. Xjunajpù, CC BY-SA 3.0 <https://creativecommons.org/licenses/by-sa/3.0>, via Wikimedia Commons: https://commons.wikimedia.org/wiki/File:Popol_Wuj%27s_deity.png

[21] Photo zoomed in. Xjunajpù, CC BY-SA 3.0 <https://creativecommons.org/licenses/by-sa/3.0>, via Wikimedia Commons: https://commons.wikimedia.org/wiki/File:Popol_Wuj%27s_deity.png

[22] Lacambalam, CC BY-SA 4.0 <https://creativecommons.org/licenses/by-sa/4.0>, via Wikimedia Commons: https://commons.wikimedia.org/wiki/File:Hero_Twins.JPG

[23] Madman2001, CC BY 3.0 <https://creativecommons.org/licenses/by/3.0>, via Wikimedia Commons: https://commons.wikimedia.org/wiki/File:Staircase_Riser,_Maya,_ballgame.jpg

[24] Sylvanus Griswold Morley, (1883-1948), Public domain, via Wikimedia Commons: https://commons.wikimedia.org/wiki/File:Maya_Hieroglyphs_Fig_39.jpg

[25] Croppy Peace Sign, CC0, via Wikimedia Commons; https://commons.wikimedia.org/wiki/File:Construction_paper_Mayan_calander.jpg

[26] Drawing by William E. Gates from the Dresden Codex, Public Domain: https://commons.wikimedia.org/wiki/File:Maize_God_and_Itzamn%C3%A1.JPG

[27] John Romkey from USA, CC BY 2.0 <https://creativecommons.org/licenses/by/2.0>, via Wikimedia Commons: https://commons.wikimedia.org/wiki/File:Chichen_Itza_ruins_in_Mexico_--_by_John_Romkey.jpg

[28] https://commons.wikimedia.org/wiki/File:01-maya-lidar-mapping.jpg

[29] *Cascajal-text.jpg: Michael Eversonderivative work: Jon C, CC BY 3.0 <https://creativecommons.org/licenses/by/3.0>, via Wikimedia Commons: https://commons.wikimedia.org/wiki/File:Cascajal-text.svg*

[30] *Madman, CC BY-SA 3.0 <http://creativecommons.org/licenses/by-sa/3.0/>, via Wikimedia Commons: https://commons.wikimedia.org/wiki/File:Monument_3,_San_Jose_Mogote.JPG*

[31] *Lacambalam, CC BY-SA 4.0 <https://creativecommons.org/licenses/by-sa/4.0>, via Wikimedia Commons: https://commons.wikimedia.org/wiki/File:Detail_of_Codex_Dresdensis_drawn_by_Lacambalam.jpg*

[32] *https://commons.wikimedia.org/wiki/File:Maya_script_reading_direction.png*

[33] *Goran tek-en, CC BY-SA 4.0 <https://creativecommons.org/licenses/by-sa/4.0>, via Wikimedia Commons: https://commons.wikimedia.org/wiki/File:Balam_3.svg*

[34] *https://commons.wikimedia.org/wiki/File:Ixchel.svg*

[35] *Shark at the Lithuanian language Wikipedia, CC BY-SA 3.0 <http://creativecommons.org/licenses/by-sa/3.0/>, via Wikimedia Commons: https://commons.wikimedia.org/wiki/File:Tikalas.jpg*

[36] *Dave Jimisonderivative work: MrPanyGoff, CC BY-SA 2.0 <https://creativecommons.org/licenses/by-sa/2.0>, via Wikimedia Commons: https://commons.wikimedia.org/wiki/File:Tikal_Temple_I.jpg*

[37] *Chaccard. Cropped by User:Andrew Dalby, CC BY-SA 4.0 <https://creativecommons.org/licenses/by-sa/4.0>, via Wikimedia Commons: https://commons.wikimedia.org/wiki/File:Codex_Fej%C3%A9v%C3%A1ry-Mayer_kapok_tree.JPG*

[38] *Greg Willis, CC BY-SA 2.0 <https://creativecommons.org/licenses/by-sa/2.0>, via Wikimedia Commons: https://commons.wikimedia.org/wiki/File:Burial_10_vessel.jpg*

[39] *Bjørn Christian Tørrissen, CC BY-SA 3.0 <https://creativecommons.org/licenses/by-sa/3.0>, via Wikimedia Commons: https://commons.wikimedia.org/wiki/File:DSC03332TikalUnderjordiskSteinansikt.JPG*

[40] *AlejandroLinaresGarcia, CC BY-SA 4.0 <https://creativecommons.org/licenses/by-sa/4.0>, via Wikimedia Commons: https://commons.wikimedia.org/wiki/File:JadeMaskTikalJadeSanCris.JPG*

[41] *https://commons.wikimedia.org/wiki/File:Maya_cranial_deformation.gif*

[42] *Photo zoomed in. Gary Todd from Xinzheng, China, CC0, via Wikimedia Commons: https://commons.wikimedia.org/wiki/File:Maya_Temple_of_the_Frescoes,_Bonampak,_Murals_Copied_by_Artist_Rina_Lazo_(9758814221).jpg*

[43] *https://commons.wikimedia.org/wiki/File:God_A_Ah_Puch_(Kimi).jpg*

[44] *Bernard DUPONT, CC BY-SA 2.0 <https://creativecommons.org/licenses/by-sa/2.0>, via Wikimedia Commons: https://commons.wikimedia.org/wiki/File:Ceramic_Funerary_Mask_..._Calakmul,_Early_Classic_(200-600_AD).jpg*

⁴⁵ Wolfgang Sauber, CC BY-SA 3.0 <https://creativecommons.org/licenses/by-sa/3.0>, via Wikimedia Commons: https://commons.wikimedia.org/wiki/File:Maya_Priester.jpg

⁴⁶ https://commons.wikimedia.org/wiki/File:Mayan_priest_smoking.jpg

⁴⁷ Luisedu mendez, CC BY-SA 3.0 <https://creativecommons.org/licenses/by-sa/3.0>, via Wikimedia Commons: https://commons.wikimedia.org/wiki/File:Fondo_maya.jpg

⁴⁸ https://www.education.com/

⁴⁹ British Museum, CC BY 3.0 <https://creativecommons.org/licenses/by/3.0>, via Wikimedia Commons: https://commons.wikimedia.org/wiki/File:Crystal_skull_british_museum_random9834672.jpg

⁵⁰ Estela Parra, CC BY-SA 4.0 <https://creativecommons.org/licenses/by-sa/4.0>, via Wikimedia Commons; https://commons.wikimedia.org/wiki/File:Mascara_de_calakmul.jpg

⁵¹ Photo zoomed in. ZuyuaT, CC BY-SA 4.0 <https://creativecommons.org/licenses/by-sa/4.0>, via Wikimedia Commons: https://commons.wikimedia.org/wiki/File:El_Castillo,_Chichen_Itza.jpg

⁵² Gary Todd, CC0, via Wikimedia Commons: https://commons.wikimedia.org/wiki/File:Classic_Maya_Clay_Figurine,_Jaina_Island,_Campeche_-_9757546556.jpg

⁵³ Gary Todd from Xinzheng, China, CC0, via Wikimedia Commons: https://commons.wikimedia.org/wiki/File:Maya_Pottery_Rabbit_(9759285271).jpg

⁵⁴ Xjunajpù, CC BY-SA 3.0 <https://creativecommons.org/licenses/by-sa/3.0>, via Wikimedia Commons: https://commons.wikimedia.org/wiki/File:Popol_Wuj%27s_deity.png

⁵⁵ https://commons.wikimedia.org/wiki/File:Cipactli.jpg

⁵⁶ Xjunajpù, CC BY-SA 3.0 <https://creativecommons.org/licenses/by-sa/3.0>, via Wikimedia Commons: https://commons.wikimedia.org/wiki/File:Jarron_Maya_1_-_Hunahp%C3%BA_e_Ixbalanqu%C3%A9.jpg

⁵⁷ Wolfgang Sauber (User:Xenophon), CC BY-SA 3.0 <https://creativecommons.org/licenses/by-sa/3.0>, via Wikimedia Commons: https://commons.wikimedia.org/wiki/File:Maya-Maske.jpg

⁵⁸ Gary Todd, CC0, via Wikimedia Commons: https://commons.wikimedia.org/wiki/File:Stone_Serpent_Head_-_Palacio_Canton.jpg

⁵⁹ https://www.education.com/

www.ingramcontent.com/pod-product-compliance
Lightning Source LLC
Chambersburg PA
CBHW070334010526
44107CB00004B/504